I0448236

Table of Contents

Executive Summary

Understanding human dynamics is an essential aspect of planning for success across the full spectrum of military and national security operations. While the adage that "warfare is political conflict by other means" is widely recognized, combatants who underestimate the impact of the human element in military operations do so at their risk. During the Second World War and the reconstruction that followed, as well as during the Cold War, understanding human dynamics was considered essential.

> As conceptualized in this report, the term **"human dynamics"** comprises the actions and interactions of personal, interpersonal, and social/contextual factors and their effects on behavioral outcomes. Human dynamics are influenced by factors such as economics, religion, politics, and culture. **Culture** is defined herein as the particular norms and beliefs held by every human, that impacts how individuals, groups and societies perceive, behave and interact.

Although, the U.S. military belatedly increased its human dynamics awareness within the current Iraq and Afghanistan theaters, recent progress has been achieved because of its importance in strategic, operational, and tactical decision-making. The U.S. military has also made recent progress in training and sensitizing deployed U.S. forces to the importance of understanding human dynamics in dealing with individuals, groups, and societies. There have been numerous, though mostly uncoordinated, efforts within DoD to manage relevant databases and provide associated tools and cultural advisors. To a large extent, these efforts recapitulate "lessons learned and since forgotten" from prior engagements—capabilities that were permitted to lapse and were no longer organic to DoD.

Substantial improvements by DoD are needed in understanding human dynamics. In particular, DoD must take a longer-term view and build upon increased capability achieved in Iraq and Afghanistan. It must institutionalize the best of current programs and processes so that this capability is also available across the full spectrum of military operations, including increased emphasis on activities, referred to as Phase 0, that seek to mitigate the likelihood of armed conflict.

To be effective in the long term, DoD must develop more coherence in its efforts to enhance human dynamics awareness. Most importantly, capability must be expanded beyond the focus of current armed conflicts so that the Department and military services have the flexibility to adjust rapidly to events in other places in the world. Playing "catch-up" will not be an effective option.

The task force believes that opportunities with both near-term and long-term payoffs exist for substantial improvement in the following areas:

- coordination and leadership

- interagency and civil interactions

- education, training, and career development

- human dynamics advisors

- science and technology investments

- data, tools, and products

Specific recommendations, grouped by the topics listed above, are presented in the balance of this summary, and are detailed in the chapters that follow. All of the recommendations presented in this report are important for conflicts the nation is likely to face in the next decade or two. However, four of them should have the highest priority in the near term, because they provide the foundations that will enable all the rest. These four priority recommendations are:

1. **Develop a comprehensive strategy**

2. **Establish effective oversight**

3. **Include specifically in upcoming Quadrennial Defense Review (QDR)**

4. **Increase the "cultural bench"**

Coordination and Leadership

There is a growing body of DoD investments in knowledge related to human dynamics, ranging from data collection and analysis to field support and training. For example, each of the U.S. armed services has programs underway to build cultural awareness for stability operations, to acquire germane data, and to use communications to enhance training and consultation. However, this disparate set of programs shows signs of duplication as well as common shortfalls. The task force found little evidence of coordination among these programs or of a long-range plan for further development and management—either among the Services, within a combatant command, or by the Office of the Secretary of Defense.

As no single repository, coordination entity, or management function exists today, the task force had great difficulty identifying all relevant, on-going efforts in human dynamics. The task force was also unable to find either a guiding strategy, or individuals or organizations that could identify all the associated efforts currently underway or previously conducted by the U.S. military. Future detailed assessments of human dynamics initiatives can build upon survey work currently ongoing in multiple quarters within DoD. However, human dynamics efforts today appear uneven and duplicative, and lack evaluative measures or even a common vocabulary.

> **"Over the long term, we cannot kill or capture our way to victory. Non-military efforts—these tools of persuasion and inspiration—were indispensable to the outcome of the defining ideological struggle of the 20th century. They are just as indispensable in the 21st century — and perhaps even more so."**
>
> *Defense Secretary Robert Gates, July 2008*

There have been successes based on careful attention to cultural influences on human dynamics. The story of El Salvador, summarized in Chapter 3, is a recent example of "best practices" in this application.

The need for understanding human dynamics will continue to be important in the foreseeable future, as the United States interacts with numerous cultures to achieve national security goals and objectives. Human dynamics capabilities are critically important for future military missions and engagements and should be treated as such. Moreover, they are often most valuable in shaping events before hostilities are underway—perhaps even preventing hostilities. The Department must avoid loss of focus and of important capabilities in this area when current engagements in Iraq and Afghanistan subside. As understanding human dynamics will continue to be of utmost importance, it should be specifically included in the upcoming QDR.

One opportunity to learn and develop human dynamics capabilities, unencumbered by the demands of major conflict, would be to establish a pilot activity within a regional combatant command. A pilot activity would offer the opportunity to develop tactics, techniques, and procedures for possible theater engagement, as well as preparation for disaster mitigation and potential stability operations. This pilot activity would also provide the opportunity to develop and test interdisciplinary and interagency relationships as well as multinational cooperation.

RECOMMENDATION 1. COORDINATION AND LEADERSHIP (CHAPTER 3)

The Secretary of Defense should:

- **Instruct his staff to develop a comprehensive strategy** that builds upon programs now underway in the Army and Marine Corps to assure human dynamics awareness for future stability operations. This strategy should also include directives on education and training, human dynamics advisors, and knowledge management, as outlined below.

- Review and determine the best course of action to **establish effective oversight and coordination** of human dynamic activities

- **Ensure that the implications for force structure and DoD appropriations** of all the recommendations of this report are considered in the upcoming QDR.

The Chairman of the Joint Chiefs should direct a regional combatant commander to develop tactics, techniques, and procedures for employing enhanced knowledge of human dynamics in anticipation of stability operations with U.S. forces in non-combatant roles, cooperating closely with other combatant commands, U.S. agencies, and non-government organizations (NGOs), as well as allies and host nations.

Interagency and Civil Organization Interactions

> "Future military challenges cannot be overcome by military means alone, and they extend well beyond the traditional domain of any single government agency or department. They require our government to operate with unity, agility, and creativity, and will require devoting considerably more resources to non-military instruments of national power."
>
> Secretary of Defense Robert M. Gates, January 26, 2008

A number of organizations beyond DoD that have expertise and experience in human dynamics of relevance to foreign cultures can and should contribute to success. These include non-government organizations, commercial industry, academia, and many government agencies other than DoD. The Department should enthusiastically develop partnerships with all.

RECOMMENDATION 2. INTERAGENCY AND CIVIL INTERACTIONS (CHAPTER 4)

The Under Secretary of Defense for Policy should:

- **Expand Unified Quest 09 exercises** to include two additional teams: private sector and non-government humanitarian organizations.

- **Review commercial approaches to human dynamics information collection and analyses** to assess relevance to the U.S. government.

- **Fund and launch the Center for Global Engagement,** recommended in a prior DSB study, to provide a centralized U.S. government interagency center for human dynamics knowledge and surge capacity.[1]

The Under Secretary of Defense for Personnel and Readiness (USD (P&R)) should increase teamwork training for military members expected to work with nongovernment organization (NGO) and private sector partners, **emphasizing coordination and cooperation skills associated with those partnerships.**

Education and Training

There has been high payoff for some of the simplest, common sense interactions with indigenous populations. Mutual respect and courtesies do not take a lot of foreign-cultural training.

The examples of Army and Marine training efforts that sought to inculcate awareness of Iraqi and Afghan culture in units preparing for deployment to Operations Iraqi Freedom and Enduring Freedom are laudable. The use of such knowledge by the 3rd Armored Cavalry Regiment (3rd ACR) in northern Iraq, the Marine Corps intelligence activity, and the Army-JIEDDO (Joint Improvised Explosive Device Defeat Organization) program at Ft. Irwin all proved to be valuable in the judgment of combat unit commanders in theater.

The Services are continuing to expand the human dynamics content of education and training curricula at their centers of excellence and academies, in their professional military education courses, and in basic training. They should be supported in doing more. Cultural insensitivity is militarily dysfunctional, especially when coupled with indiscriminate violence directed at noncombatants. Military training should persistently stress discretion in the use of force. This must be done with a clear recognition of the tensions between this discretion and effectiveness of combat power

---

1. *Report of the Defense Science Board Task Force on Strategic Communication*, January 2008.

Establishing a separate DoD social science institute would probably not contribute much to fostering cultural awareness in the armed services. However, an interagency training center for preparing teams of government and NGO representatives for stability operations, such as Provincial Reconstruction Teams, would contribute much to preparation for future engagements. Such a center would provide both socio-cultural knowledge and human dynamics astuteness. It would also foster interagency participation and enable the Army to return a prime unit (the 1st Brigade Combat Team (1st BCT), 1st Infantry Division (1st ID)) to combat operations.

RECOMMENDATION 3. EDUCATION & TRAINING (CHAPTER 5)

The Secretary of Defense should instruct his staff to undertake the following:

- **Initiate inter-departmental action** to establish, with congressional support, an **Institute for Public Administration Training** with a faculty of military experts, skilled engineers, public safety advisors, medics, social scientists, and NGO representatives, tasked (1) to assist the Services and civil participants with readiness for catastrophe relief and stability operations, and (2) to form and train multi-disciplinary teams for augmentation of any U.S. country team.

- Invite participation of interagency and NGO representatives in **mission readiness exercises**, at least by telephone consultation during planning and in after-action review.

- Direct the Defense Information Systems Agency (DISA) to bring to bear **a comprehensive set of collaborative services** that facilitate expert discovery, cross-domain security, and community creation to advance the human dynamics capabilities and cultural awareness efforts of the armed services and of the Institute for Public Administration Training.

- Support the Services in modifying the standard curriculum at U.S. military academies, as well as service-specific curricula, to incorporate **basic training in human dynamics.**

Human Dynamics Advisors

DoD personnel that provide socio-cultural expertise, such as Foreign Area Officers (FAOs), are currently spread too thin to assure adequate consideration of these matters in planning and execution. However, to offset this deficit, both the Army and the Air Force reported that each maintained an extensive network of expert cultural consultants. The combatant commands also have their own "rolodex files."

Some of the difficulties encountered with respect to using advisors include: outdated and insufficient training of military personnel and key advisors in the area of human dynamics, particularly with respect to cultural studies, dynamic network analysis, and human dynamic models and simulations; lack of attractive career paths for military personnel in the human dynamics area; and lack of procedures, funding lines, and automated expert finder/locator for effectively engaging and leveraging expertise in industry and academia.

Academia, NGOs, and commercial operations have considerable expertise in human dynamics and are strongly motivated to continuously improve their expertise, as they seek to help and/or sell to all, friend and foe alike. The Department does not currently optimize use of these capabilities, which could augment military capabilities during operations and offer greater depth of human dynamics understanding. Recognizing the importance of such cross-disciplinary interactions, Secretary Gates is actively working to reassure those who may be reluctant to collaborate with the Department of Defense and to build partnerships between DoD and other U.S. government departments and agencies in order to build a "whole-of-government" solution to challenging multi-disciplinary issues.

RECOMMENDATION 4. HUMAN DYNAMICS ADVISORS (CHAPTER 5)

The Chairman, Joint Chiefs of Staff and the Under Secretary of Defense for Personnel and Readiness, with advice from the combatant commands, should direct increases in the "cultural bench" by factors of three to five:

- Expand curriculum in this area for **professional military education.**

- Improve **career paths** for human dynamics advisors.

- Provide relevant advanced degree education.

- Develop innovative processes for **recruiting and rewarding** human dynamic expertise.

- Increase the number of **Foreign Area Officers** and assign them more effectively.

- Establish **medium- and long-term requirements** for each combatant command.

USD (P&R) should work with the Services and combatant commands to combine and augment the separate pools of available consultants, expert in particular cultures. The Assistant Secretary of Defense for Networks and Information Integration (ASD (NII)) should facilitate their connectivity and collaboration, both among themselves and with users.

Science and Technology Investments

DoD investments in human dynamics knowledge and capability were difficult for the task force to quantify because major efforts are funded by distributed sources other than research, development, test, and evaluation (RDT&E) accounts, such as operations and maintenance. Current science and technology (S&T) investments appear to be focused principally in four areas: (1) language, (2) human and cultural studies, (3) dynamic network analysis and social networks, and (4) human dynamics computational modeling and simulation.

The technologies and scientific infrastructure for language and social networks analysis have the highest degree of theoretical development within DoD. These have provided tools and models at high levels of technical readiness—although, in many cases, they have not been field-tested adequately. On the other hand, the areas of human and cultural studies, as well as modeling and simulation are less well developed within DoD. The task force used gap analysis to identify critical investment areas and recommends such analysis as an important tool to aid in the development of a roadmap and investment strategy for the future.

The task force's preliminary analysis identified key gaps in human dynamics knowledge that included:

- multi-domain, multi-speaker spoken conversation, transcription, and translation

- technologies for extracting knowledge from databases (of both structured and unstructured sources) in a way that can be used to inform and validate dynamic network models

- automated assessment of the human terrain with emphasis on attitudes, influence networks, and the effects of strategic communication

- gaming for virtual training and mission rehearsal

- automated sentiment, intention, deception detection

- geo-spatial dynamic network analysis and the combination of neuro-cognitive models and dynamic network analysis in the area of influence, attitudes, and beliefs

- open architecture state-of-the-art platforms for data, model, and tool integration

RECOMMENDATION 5. SCIENCE AND TECHNOLOGY INVESTMENTS (CHAPTER 6)

The Director, Defense Research and Engineering (DDR&E) should establish a "portfolio manager" in human dynamics covering areas such as language; socio-cultural, dynamic network analysis; and human dynamics computational modeling and simulation to track tools, models, data, and experts. The responsibilities of the portfolio manager should include the following:

- **Define and develop a road map** based on a refined gap analysis, coordinated with users—combatant commands and services. This roadmap should include a credible S&T budget and program.

- **DDR&E should perform an in-depth review of ongoing S&T programs** in this area (regardless of their budget authorities) and assess their potential based on data.

- **Define and implement a more robust research effort** to explore the potential of relevant S&T efforts in cross-cutting human dynamics research linking dynamic network analysis to findings and models with direct military relevance.

Databases, Tools, and Products

A large number of human dynamics databases exist, but they are independent of each other and have been created for specific elements of the DoD community. Furthermore, no common formats, metadata, or ontology have been established. The majority of these databases are not maintained, fully populated, or interoperable. Access is generally limited, and interaction with these databases is usually tailored to the particular users, making them of limited utility to others.

Basic social network analysis tools within DoD are mature and do not need to be reinvented. However, insufficient data, analytic tools, and modeling support are available to DoD on social structure, culture, attitudes, opinion trends, beliefs, and behaviors to enable both tactical and strategic analyses. Furthermore, the existing human dynamics databases and tools lack interoperability and employ no standards or metrics for model validation.

Some data, such as those related to trends, attitudes, and beliefs, are difficult to extract from open source documents, are proprietary and held by corporations that conduct polls, or do not exist in regions or at levels of granularity necessary for operations. Data needed for models and simulation are not routinely collected to enable baseline or trend analysis, or when collected are not shared even among the different Services, let alone with the intelligence community or non-government organizations. While such data are needed to support missions by providing (1) accurate up-to-date awareness of culture, (2) information on opinion leaders and political and military elite, and (3) dynamic social networks, much background knowledge associated with long-term trends can populate databases.

The Distributed Common Ground Station should host the cultural databases for all DoD, as well as for partners in the Department of State and U.S. AID, but standards and means will have to be developed to govern data entry, search, and retrieval, as well as dissemination. DISA's Defense Connect On-Line (DCO) can provide tools to support both training for and conduct of military operations carried out among populations. DCO could also support participation in training and operations through web conferencing for non-DoD officials and NGO representatives. Recent efforts, such as the Director of National Intelligence's "A-Space," provide a potential design model.[2]

RECOMMENDATION 6. DATABASES, TOOLS, AND PRODUCTS (CHAPTER 7)

The Secretary of Defense should direct his staff to ensure interoperable databases. Actions should include:

- Review current and historic human dynamics data collection and database efforts for the extent to which they meet military need at the tactical, operational, and strategic levels.

- Design a suitable, distributed enterprise architecture, to allow user-friendly and rapid access to all databases, including the ability to share data among various databases in response to user queries, as appropriate.

- Promulgate standards for formats, evolving ontology, update schedules and processes, and maintenance procedures.

---

2. A-Space is a project of the Office of the Director of National Intelligence to develop a common collaborative workspace for all analysts within the Intelligence Community. Accessible from common workstations, the aim of the project is to provide access to interagency databases, a capability to search classified sources and the Internet simultaneously, web-based e-mail, and other collaboration tools.

- Enforce these standards and promote buy-in from the community stakeholders inside and outside of DoD.

ASD (NII) should consolidate the databases germane to foreign culture and other human-dynamics-relevant areas into the Distributed Common Ground Station with appropriate provisions for collection, storage, retrieval, and dissemination at several levels of security.

The Under Secretary of Defense for Policy and the Under Secretary of Defense for Intelligence should increase efforts to collect human dynamics data and prepare these products so that information can be made available to multiple users. Actively engage departments and agencies government-wide as well as commercial and NGO resources and capabilities in the collection and use of data and preparation of products.

USD (P&R) should ensure that there is a sufficient cadre of individuals with human dynamics astuteness to interpret the data and products.

Combatant commanders should direct population of these databases with regional information, generating requirements for data collection and for product preparation and evaluation. They should provide guidance, support, and resources (*e.g.* expertise and data collection technology) to forces deployed in their areas for documentation of short-term history.

Collectively, these recommendations will set the Department on a path toward enhancing the human dynamics capabilities within the military services, thereby better preparing our men and women in uniform for the operational environment of the future where knowledge and understanding of others will be a critical aspect of national   security.

Chapter 1. Introduction

Among defense professionals, the "war on terrorism" and American interventions in Iraq and Afghanistan have returned to prominence issues of "human dynamics," "culture," and "the human terrain." The United States faces actual and potential challenges from adversaries who differ from us in significant ways in the human and social dimension. Moreover, in an era in which insurgency and "irregular warfare" have once again come to the fore, the U.S. military realizes that it must also understand the human environment and dynamics in the entire engagement space—including civilians, neutrals, allies, and even our own forces. It is becoming increasingly clear that the requirement for such understanding obtains not merely during hostilities, but also during peacetime in order to reduce the likelihood of armed conflict, and during the transition to and from hostilities.

What is Human Dynamics?

> In this report, **human dynamics** is defined as the actions and interactions of personal, interpersonal, and social/contextual factors and their effects on behavioral outcomes. Human dynamics are influenced by factors such as economics, religion, politics, and culture.

Understanding "human dynamics" entails several things. At the most technical level, it encompasses the actual or potential application of psychology, sociology, and anthropology, and potentially cognitive sciences, neuroscience, computer science, and other such fields. It also requires knowledge of "culture."[3]

---

3. No single definition of culture exists in the Department of Defense, as the task force came to understand during the course of its deliberations. Appendix A delineates many definitions gleaned from the briefings received and background materials reviewed by the task force.

> **Culture** is defined herein as the collection of particular norms, beliefs, and customs held by every human, that impacts how individuals, groups, and societies behave and interact.

Every interaction between an American and another person in the engagement space has cultural overtones. Given the compression of the tactical, operational, and strategic levels of war—a phenomenon encapsulated in the term "the strategic corporal"—"culture" must be something that everyone in the Defense Department "gets."[4] Soldiers, sailors, airmen, and marines who are oblivious to the influence of culture on human dynamics will not understand what they are seeing and will either miss important signals relevant to conduct of operations or flood their leadership with irrelevant or erroneous information. More dangerously, actions taken in ignorance or miscalculation can result in mission failure and perhaps loss of life.

Scope of the Study

These considerations led the Under Secretaries of Defense for Policy and for Acquisition, Technology, and Logistics (USD (AT&L)) to direct the formation of this Defense Science Board Task Force on Understanding Human Dynamics. The terms of reference call on this task force to:[5]

- review efforts to assess social structures, cultures, and behaviors of populations and adversaries

- identify and assess relevant science and technology investment plans and identify promising new opportunities

- recommend steps to accelerate the military's use of relevant knowledge and technologies in order to achieve operational capabilities

---

4. See, for instance, the new FM 3-24, Counterinsurgency (The U.S. Army/Marine Corps Counterinsurgency Field Manual).

5. The complete terms of reference, task force membership, and presentations to the task force can be found at the conclusion of this report.

Understanding human dynamics is relevant at all levels of national security from the tactical to the strategic. Nevertheless, this task force did not attempt to conduct a definitive review of the place of human dynamics in the defense community in all its breadth and depth. Rather, it chose to address primarily the consideration of this issue at the tactical and operational levels. It did so not merely to make the task feasible within the time allotted, but also because it judged that the challenge of bringing human dynamics understanding to the tactical and operational levels was greater than the corresponding challenge at the strategic level. Furthermore, the task force judged that the conclusions reached through this assessment of the tactical and operational levels would largely be directly applicable at the strategic level as well.

This task force bounded its work in two other important ways. First, it did not review any intelligence programs pertaining to human dynamics. Indeed, most of the programs examined were unclassified. Second, the task force excluded from consideration issues pertaining purely to "strategic communication," because several recent DSB studies have dealt in detail with that topic.[6] Nevertheless, strategic communication is clearly an endeavor that is profoundly affected by knowledge (or ignorance) of human dynamics and culture. For instance, the U.S. military must also understand that its actions communicate its values (sometimes accurately, sometimes not) to all communities within which they are deployed. This is true across the full spectrum of military operations, from before, during, and after use of lethal force to the distribution of humanitarian aid during disaster mitigation.

Lessons of History

Even a cursory review of past wars and conflicts shows that all military operations have a critical human dimension. What is perhaps less obvious, is how broadly influential—and often variant—are the human dynamics that shape the disposition of the population and character of conflict. Past experiences have shown that knowing an

---

6. See *Report of the Defense Science Board Task Force on Strategic Communication,* January 2008; *Report of the Defense Science Board Task Force on Strategic Communication,* September 2004; and *Report of the Defense Science Board Task Force on Managed Information Dissemination,* October 2001.

enemy may be important, but knowing the population and the broader "battle space" context may be equally so.[7]

Past experiences have shown that knowing an enemy may be important, but knowing the population and the broader "battle space" context may be equally so.

The U.S. military has invested in human dynamics understanding when previously fighting irregular or unconventional adversaries—during the Philippine War (once called the Philippine Insurrection) and the Vietnam War, for instance. On both occasions, the military came to the cultural game late and then, when the conflict was over, turned its back on the subject as part of a conscious effort to put behind an unpleasant experience. As former Vice Chief of Staff of the Army, General Jack Keane, lamented in the context of Iraq, "after the Vietnam War, we purged ourselves of everything that had to do with irregular warfare or insurgency, because it had to do with how we lost that war."[8]

The U.S. entry into Afghanistan and its early victories over the Taliban were accomplished largely by U.S. Special Forces working with indigenous tribal forces whose motives and leadership were understood. Our military belatedly adapted to the human dynamics needs of the war in Iraq and the more recent situation in Afghanistan. But whatever the outcome of these present conflicts, this knowledge, both of substance and with respect to the importance of human dynamics, must not be allowed to slip away once again. The U.S. military must embrace the fact that human dynamics and war are now and forever inextricably intertwined.[9]

---

7. Appendix B contains discussion of past experiences with human dynamics in military operations and identifies insights drawn from those experiences.

8. Keane is quoted in Shawn Brimley and Vikram Singh, "Averting the System Reboot," *Armed Forces Journal*, http://www.armedforcesjournal.com/2007/12/2981245, accessed 26 June 2008. With regard to Vietnam, see also, notably, Andrew F. Krepinevich, Jr., *The Army and Vietnam*, (Baltimore: Johns Hopkins University Press, 1986). With respect to the Philippines, see, *e.g.* Brian McAllister Linn, "Intelligence and Low-Intensity Conflict in the Philippine War, 1899–1902," *Intelligence and National Security*, 6:1 (1991), pp. 90–114.

9. Among those military historians who focused on insurgency and counterinsurgency, this has never been news. It is now also widely accepted that "conventional" wars are also deeply pervaded and influenced by cultural considerations. This interpretive revolution began more than thirty years ago. See, perhaps most notably, John Keegan, *The Face of Battle* (New York: Viking Press, 1976) and *A History of Warfare*, (New York: Alfred A. Knopf, 1993); Victor Davis

The above message may appear disheartening to some, but it should not. An understanding of human dynamics does not merely help prevent the U.S. military from losing. It can, in fact, help the military win its future wars more surely and decisively, particularly asymmetric encounters such as counterinsurgency and counterterrorism campaigns. It may even prevent the United States from having to fight in the first place.

... the importance of human dynamics, must not be allowed to slip away once again. The U.S. military must embrace the fact that human dynamics and war are now and forever inextricably intertwined.

Understanding human dynamics can also allow the U.S. military to work more smoothly with its partners and to mitigate conflicts more effectively. Knowledge of the value system of an actual or potential competitor helps in deterring undesirable behaviors and compelling desirable behaviors. Preliminary experience with human terrain approaches suggests that during hostilities, a commander who understands the human terrain in which his unit is operating will find that unit subject to less friction, under less force-protection threat, receiving more intelligence tips from the population, and probably inflicting less collateral damage.

It is important that members of the American military understand their own culture and the ways in which it influences human dynamics. By its very nature, an individual's culture is largely unconscious, stemming from a collection of beliefs and behaviors the individual often takes for granted without constant reassessment. However, understanding what defines one's own culture can help one to understand foreign cultures and vice versa. For example, a member of the U.S. military may assume that others share his or her beliefs about "equality" or "democracy;" that a lack of punctuality is a sign of disrespect or laziness; and that his or her good intentions as an American soldier, sailor, airman, or marine, are self-evident. Often these

Hanson, *The Western Way of War: Infantry Battle in Classical Greece*, (New York, Alfred A. Knopf, 1989) and *Carnage and Culture: Landmark Battles in the Rise of Western Power*, (New York: Doubleday, 2001); Kenneth Pollack, *Arabs at War: Military Effectiveness, 1948-1991*, (Lincoln: University of Nebraska Press, 2002); and John Lynn Battle: *A History of Combat and Culture*, (Boulder: Westview Press, 2003).

are good assumptions. At other times, they are dangerously inappropriate.

An understanding of human dynamics is important to operators and analysts during peacetime as well as wartime

An understanding of human dynamics is important to operators and analysts during peacetime as well as wartime. For example, culturally-rooted disputes can lead to the outbreak of hostilities, which may require the commitment of American forces where none were present before. By the same token, if American forces are present in a foreign country during peacetime, culturally insensitive actions or words by even one individual can engender hostility and violence.

While it may be presumptuous to conclude that there are definitive and invariant "lessons" that have been or should have been learned from past experiences, there are certainly insights that are worth consideration:

- Awareness of human dynamics facilitates strategic and tactical success.

- It is necessary to understand and accept that military operations have political objectives and effects.

- Populations matter as much as fighting forces in determining military success.

- Continuity of knowledge on human dynamics is essential, as personnel change and units rotate, particularly in joint/coalition and protracted operations.

- Human dynamics may vary across and within conflicts or operations.

As Major General (Retired) Robert H. Scales has so eloquently observed based on past experiences, "Wars are won as much by creating alliances, leveraging nonmilitary advantages, reading intentions, building trust, converting opinions, and managing perceptions—all these tasks demand an exceptional ability to understand people, their culture, and their motivation."[10]

---

10. Scales, Robert H. (2004). "Culture-Centric Warfare," *Proceedings*, 130(9), p.3.

Chapter 2. The Importance of Human Dynamics in Future U.S. Military Operations

The complexity of the national security environment in the early 21st century requires the U.S. military to anticipate and be fully prepared to respond to a wide range of contingencies. Whether called upon to conduct limited intervention, irregular warfare, major combat operations, stability operations, peacetime engagement, humanitarian missions, or civil support, each contingency presents the U.S. military with significant additional challenges associated with its proximity to populations. A deep understanding of human dynamics will be needed to avert armed conflict wherever possible and to effectively and efficiently respond to emerging security conditions.

Characteristics of Future Operations

"... whether prompted by cooperation, competition or conflict, future joint operations will require far greater cultural awareness than U.S. forces have demonstrated before."

Capstone Concept for Joint Operations, Jan 2009

Future military operations will likely differ from those in the past in a number of ways. They will be more fluid and more complex, the pace of operations will be higher, the importance of non-kinetic tools will increase, the operating space will be closer to centers of population, and the need for information will expand exponentially. Each of these characteristics will require extended awareness of the human dimension.

The national security environment will be multi-dimensional with strong roots in human dynamics. The operational environment will include the air, land, maritime, space, and cyber domains, and will be affected by nonmilitary operational variables influenced by local populations. Joint planners consider this environment in terms of six variables, all of which encompass human dynamics to some degree: political, military, economic, social, information,   and   infrastructure.

Full spectrum operations will add to the complexity and variability of U.S. military operations. The complexity of full spectrum operations, as well as deterrence and humanitarian missions will be driven in part by an operational environment that simultaneously includes elements of conventional war, guerilla warfare, and terrorism. To deter and defeat such challenges, the U.S. military must have the expeditionary capability to deploy forces any time, any geography, and for any type of contingency, and to simultaneously combine offense, defense, and stability operations, often in extended proximity to populations. Coordination and collaboration between U.S. departments and agencies, multinational partners, and civil authorities will be critical to success.

Operational tempo will increase in response to the pace of events in a networked world. Events in the diplomatic, informational, military, and economic spheres continue to evolve at an increasing rate of speed. Increased responsiveness from U.S. military capabilities will be required in order to retain initiative and to capitalize on emerging opportunities. Maintaining an awareness of information, misinfor-

Military operations will more frequently occur among populations...

mation, and communication flows will be an ongoing challenge, adding to the complexity of U.S. military operations. Non-state actors are becoming increasingly sophisticated through the use of distributed leadership (and sometimes even leaderless organizations) over networked communications. This networked environment will present a long-term organizational challenge to U.S. interests.

Non-kinetic military operations based on engagement will increase in importance. A new concept of strategic deterrence is emerging in terms of the theory and practice appropriate to a range of anticipated state and nontraditional threats. Future conflict should not be expected to be resolved by military forces alone, but will require the coordination of diplomatic, informational, military, and economic efforts that are constructive and non-lethal. It will involve important elements of long-term risk mitigation, such as capacity building, humanitarian assistance, expansion of regional frameworks to improve governance, cooperation to enforce the rule of law, and training and support to indigenous forces.

Military operations will more frequently be conducted among populations. The range of anticipated contingencies and adversaries will increasingly require deployment of U.S. military forces among populations, rather than isolated across defined military-military lines. Transitions between lethal and non-lethal actions will be expected of small teams operating within these populations. The ability of all U.S. echelons to distinguish between—and appropriately engage with—adversaries, competitors, neutrals, and friends will require varying degrees of cross-cultural awareness, competence, and astuteness.

Unified action will link joint, interagency, intergovernmental, and multinational capabilities in new ways. The scope and complexity of stability operations, reconstruction, and humanitarian efforts will require the U.S. military to operate in partnership with other organizations, both governmental and non-government. Joint U.S. military forces will need to work with other U.S. government departments and agencies, allies, non-governmental organizations, contractors, and civilians. Achieving cooperation and unity of effort between and among such diverse organizations will be a human dynamics challenge for individuals throughout all echelons.

Civil-military cooperation will increase in importance. The civil situation, including civil security and civil control, restoration of essential services, support to governance, and support to economic and infrastructure development, will be considered along with offensive and defense operations. In a stressed, failing, or disaster-stricken state, the U.S. military may need to work with civilian agencies of that state to establish basic capabilities and provide support to the local population.

Information engagement requirements will significantly expand. In an era where populations are linked by instant communications, information will also shape the operational environment. Information engagement can communicate critical knowledge, build trust, promote support for U.S. operations, and influence the perceptions and behaviors of many audiences. It places a high premium on understanding the local political, social, and economic situation within an area of operation. It also requires access to detailed information and trends regarding relevant audiences and their respective cultures, interests, and objectives. A sophisticated understanding of traditional media (print, radio, and video broadcasting), social media (*e.g.* wiki, blogs), collaborative media, as well as influence networks will be necessary for audience understanding, tracking, and influence. Ongoing data collection will be needed to identify emerging issues and opportunities that will serve as essential underpinnings of U.S. government strategic communication and public diplomacy efforts.

Human Dynamics Requirements

Human dynamics astuteness combines cultural, historical, and linguistic understanding, with the ability to work across organizational lines, both inside and outside the U.S. government. It recognizes that the skills of partnership development essential to joint, interagency, intergovernmental, and multinational operations will become as critical to mission accomplishment as those of command and control leadership.

For optimal effectiveness, U.S. military operators will also require extended awareness of diplomatic, information, military, economic, and other elements that underpin the intent, will, and ability of both the United States and potential adversaries to conduct military operations. A deeper understanding of the attitudes and actions of civilian populations at home and abroad will also be important.

Military leaders, planners, and operators will need greater human dynamics aptitudes to be effective in the future operational environment. … "Engagement, relationship, and strategic partnership are as important as being strong."

Building and strengthening relationships with allies, improving ties to emerging partners, and a better understanding of potential competitors will be important as well. As the Chairman, Joint Chiefs of Staff has stated, "Engagement, relationship and strategic partnership are as important as being strong."[11]

Findings Relevant to Human Dynamics Capabilities

In preparation for the likely range of future U.S. military operations, the following capabilities should be enhanced so that DoD's leadership, as well as deployed forces, will possess the necessary aptitudes, experience, and support to achieve success:

- **Enhanced granularity of strategic, operational, and tactical human dynamics knowledge**—including political, military, economic, social, and infrastructure baseline facts and trends throughout the world—will be needed to maintain an effective portfolio of contingency plans in advance of future military operations.

- A clearly defined and understandable definition of human dynamics and culture is essential to coordinating the multitude of research, operational, and intelligence efforts, to avoid undue replication of effort and to achieve improvements in collection, analysis, and dissemination of products. The current definition of "culture," found in the *DoD Dictionary of Military and Associated Terms* (Joint Publication 1-02), does not characterize human dynamics in a useful context.[12]

- **Human dynamics knowledge should be an integral part of the planning process** and incorporated in developing a portfolio of contingency plans in advance of the need for such plans.

- **Cross-cultural awareness and astuteness of commanders, as well as soldiers, sailors, airmen, and marines** can be achieved through changes in education, training, foreign language acquisition, and career development.

---

11. Chairman, Joint Chiefs of Staff, March 2008 Pentagon Town Hall Meeting.
12. In that dictionary, culture is defined as, "A feature of the terrain that has been constructed by man. Included are such items as roads, buildings, and canals; boundary lines; and, in a broad sense, all names and legends on a map."

- **A cadre of on-call human dynamics and civil affairs experts** could provide supplemental knowledge and capacity for contingency planning, as well as for strategic, operational, and tactical phases of mission management. These experts would bring in-depth functional knowledge, along with detailed experience in the area of concern.

- **Non-U.S. military organizations, nongovernmental organizations, and international organizations should be included** in the process of collecting and analyzing information on human dynamics. Importantly, these analytic assets do not have to be assigned to an intelligence organization.

- **The emphasis should be on human dynamics "products"** in addition to centralized databases and supposed systems. Products, as recommended by Colonel H.R. McMaster in Iraq, can be envisioned at three levels:

  - **"World view" documents** (*e.g.*, country handbooks) provide a basic overview of a country, region, or culture. With respect to human dynamics, these documents should include perspectives of factions (tribes, clans, villages), fears, aspirations, prejudices, and beliefs of local populations.

  - **Micro-history of the region** to include deep and narrow, updated information concerning rivalries, smuggling routes, nature of external support, and other relevant information. Language proficiency and cultural, political, and economic expertise is required to prepare these products.

  - **Short-term operational assessments** prepared by units departing an area to aid the incoming units in assessing the area and for continuity of operations. A standard format and content outline should be developed that includes details of successes and especially of failures in dealing with the populace.

- **Education and training are critical** to the delivery of useful information on human dynamics:

  - Language proficiency and cultural awareness are needed as part of the professional military education process with a phased approach recognizing a service member's rank and occupational specialty.

- Instruction should be delivered to the greatest extent possible by persons who have relevant depth of knowledge and recent experience in the operational environment being discussed.

- **Depth of knowledge about diverse audiences and the complex range of information exchange in which they participate** will increase in importance to future military operations, as the criticality of the information environment is recognized by both adversaries and allies.

- **Advances in social, cognitive, and neurological science may offer insights into human behavior,** which academia, the private sector, the U.S. government, and its allies and adversaries can all be anticipated to explore.

- Enhanced human dynamics astuteness that integrates region-specific knowledge with the ability to coordinate and cooperate across organizational lines will become key to successful future military operations that are joint, interagency, intergovernmental, or multinational, and may also include public/ private partnerships with civil society.

The remaining chapters of this report address these findings and offer recommendations that, collectively, will set the Department on a path toward enhancing the human dynamics capabilities within the military services, thereby better preparing our men and women in uniform for the operational environment of the future.

Chapter 3. Coordination and Leadership

After five years in Afghanistan and Iraq, the U.S. military services understand the lessons learned by their predecessors engaged in similar operations. During operations the host population has to be regarded as an invaluable source of information on adversaries. The community needs to be treated in a manner that avoids overt hostility and obtains cooperation. Force needs to be used with the greatest of discipline. Such an approach serves the traditional American objective beyond armed conflict: to convert our most bitter enemies into friends and allies.

A determined enemy, embedded in a foreign population, cannot be deterred or disrupted solely with advanced technology or indiscriminate coercion.

In February 2008, General Casey, Chief of Staff of the Army, presented to his generals a revision of Field Manual 3-0, *Operations*, the foreword of which states: "This edition of FM 3-0, the first update since September 11, 2001, is a revolutionary departure from past doctrine. It describes an operational concept where commanders employ offensive, defensive, and stability or civil support operations simultaneously as part of an interdependent joint force to seize, retain, and exploit the initiative, accepting prudent risk to create opportunities to achieve decisive results."[13]

"Doctrine" is best understood as an operative term: what we collectively believe about the best way to conduct military affairs. It is persistently taught in training to assure the consensus, which in combat facilitates cooperation among components of a force. For example, U.S. doctrine has consistently fostered recognition that killing prisoners of war is dysfunctional. It is not only contrary to the Uniform Code and international norms, but also incites an adversary to do likewise and negates a useful source of intelligence. The previous edition of FM 3-0, dated June 2001—written in an era of preoccupation with "overwhelming force" and "shock and awe"—emphasized *domination*, characterizing land combat as "contact with the enemy throughout the

---

13. http://www.army.mil/fm3-0.pdf

depth of an operational area…maneuver, fires, and other elements of combat power intended to defeat or destroy enemy forces." It did note, however, that "land combat normally entails close and continuous contact with noncombatants. Rules of engagement reflect this."

Use of the word "contact" to equate to "defeat or destroy," on the one hand, and to "rules that temper actions toward people of the locale," on the other hand, failed to address the circumstances of current and likely future operations. To defeat or destroy an adversary he must first be found, and rules for engagement once we find him (or he finds us) scarcely address the importance of the role the populace could play in the "finding." In contrast, the current FM 3-0 enjoins commanders to go beyond defining "rules of engagement" to integrating their objectives for the populace into their plans and operations for achieving and sustaining stability (see sidebar, *Army Field Manual 3-0*).

Importantly, it recognizes the modern 24/7 news cycle, citizen reporter, ubiquity of surveillance, and global communications (*e.g.*, many players "will have satellites or their own unmanned aerial reconnaissance platforms"). This implies an increased requirement for cultural sensitivity, and partnership with local populations.

U.S land forces have not always done well in such complicated circumstances, particularly when the national mood was vengeful, as it has been since September 11, 2001 during the global war on terrorism. Many military critics have warned against expecting that technology alone will enable elite, specialized units to control populations and large expanses of land.[14] They are right, and the Gulf wars must be regarded as an aberration in that the population did not play an important role in American operations that were designed to destroy the Iraqi Army.

---

14. See, for example, Sir Michael Howard (1994) "How Much Can Technology Change War?" and H.R. McMaster (2008). http://www.strategicstudiesinstitute.army.mil/pubs/ display.cfm?pubID=354. "On War: Lessons to be Learned," *Survival*, 50:1, 19–30. [Howard warned against military lessons drawn from history: usually "bad history and worse logic."]

Army Field Manual 3-0. Excerpts

1-11.   In essence, the operational environment of the future will still be an arena in which bloodshed is the immediate result of hostilities between antagonists. It will also be an arena in which operational goals are attained or lost not only by the use of highly lethal force but also by how quickly a state of stability can be established and maintained. The operational environment will remain a dirty, frightening, physically and emotionally draining one in which death and destruction result from environmental conditions creating humanitarian crisis as well as conflict itself. Due to the extremely high lethality and range of advanced weapons systems, and the tendency of adversaries to operate among the population, the risk to combatants and noncombatants will be much greater. All adversaries, state or non-state, regardless of technological or military capability, can be expected to use the full range of options, including every political, economic, informational, and military measure at their disposal. In addition, the operational environment will expand to areas historically immune to battle, including the continental United States and the territory of multinational partners, especially urban areas. In fact, the operational environment will probably include areas not defined by geography, such as cyberspace. Computer network attacks will span borders and will be able to hit anywhere, anytime. With the exception of cyberspace, all operations will be conducted "among the people" and outcomes will be measured in terms of effects on populations.

1-12.   The operational environment will be extremely fluid, with continually changing coalitions, alliances, partnerships, and actors. Interagency and joint operations will be required to deal with this wide and intricate range of players occupying the environment. International news organizations, using new information and communications technologies, will no longer have to depend on states to gain access to the area of operations and will greatly influence how operations are viewed. They will have satellites or their own unmanned aerial reconnaissance platforms from which to monitor the scene. Secrecy will be difficult to maintain, making operations security more vital than ever. Finally, complex cultural, demographic, and physical environmental factors will be present, adding to the fog of war. Such factors include humanitarian crises, ethnic and religious differences, and complex and urban terrain, which often become major centers of gravity and a haven for potential threats. The operational environment will be interconnected, dynamic, and extremely volatile.

In recent history, stability and reconstruction efforts all too often have been undercut by instances of cultural ignorance and military oppression: undisciplined violence and even barbarism such as occurred at My Lai in 1968. In 2008, forty years after My Lai, Secretary Gates commented ruefully on more recent dysfunctional behavior of some American troops: "In Iraq and Afghanistan, the heroic efforts and best intentions of our men and women in uniform have at times been undercut by a lack of knowledge of the culture and people they are dealing with every day—societies organized by networks of kin and tribe, where ancient codes of shame and honor often mean a good deal more than 'hearts and minds' ..."[15]

Cultural insensitivity among U.S. forces is neither peculiar to the present conflict, nor has it always been caused by unexpected encounters with foreign cultures. In 1863, President Lincoln ordered promulgation of General Order Number 100 to temper the propensity of some of his commanders to tolerate the very sort of disorders that Secretary Gates deplored.[16]

> **Art. 68. "Modern wars are not internecine wars, in which the killing of the enemy is the object ..."**
>
> *President Abraham Lincoln, 1863*

On the other hand, American forces have shown that, properly led, acting in concert with other agencies of the United States, and amply resourced, they can successfully conduct low-intensity conflict (stability operations). Secretary Gates himself, in a previous office as Deputy Director of Central Intelligence, participated in one such success, cited approvingly in 1988 by the Commission on Integrated Long-Term Strategy:

> "Low intensity conflict [is] a form of conflict that is not a problem just for the Department of Defense. In many situations, the

---

15. http://www.defenselink.mil/speeches/speech.aspx?speechid=1228
16. http://www.yale.edu/lawweb/avalon/lieber.htm. *Instructions for the Government of Armies of the United States in the Field.* Prepared by Francis Lieber, LLD. Promulgated by President Lincoln, 24 April 1863. That General Order constituted a landmark in establishing what is now termed the Laws of War. The belligerents during the Franco-Prussian War of 1871 adopted its tenets, and the United States republished G.O. 100 during the Spanish-American War; it figured prominently in American jurisprudence during the Philippine Insurgency. *Plus ca change, plus c'est la meme chose.*

United States will need not just DoD personnel and material, but diplomats and information specialists, agricultural chemists, bankers and economists, hydrologists, criminologists, meteorologists, and scores of other professionals. Because so many Americans are predisposed to pessimism about our role in the Third World, it is worth pointing to one recent example of a U.S. intervention that, against high odds, did very well: the saving of democracy in El Salvador. In 1980 it seemed quite possible that the country would fall to guerillas supported from Nicaragua by the Sandinistas and Cubans. Many Americans assumed that the [Salvadoran] government would soon be toppled by the Communist insurgents. Congress severely limited the security assistance our government could make available to it. And yet by 1985 there was a democratic government in place in El Salvador, and Congress became committed to supporting it."[17]

By agreement with the Congress, American military forces on the ground in El Salvador, other than individuals assigned to the Embassy, were limited to 55. These were foreclosed from direct participation in combat, and confined to training the Salvadoran armed forces to: (1) limit the ability of the guerillas to move freely through the countryside in their depredations, and (2) observe, when interacting with the populace, strict rules for respect of human rights. Those Americans, assigned by the Commander, U.S. Southern Command,[18] were largely drawn from units of the Army's Special Forces that were linguistically and culturally prepared to instruct and to motivate Salvadorans, supplemented by Spanish-speaking technicians, such as communicators, medics, and one U.S. Southern Command sociologist.

Perhaps more importantly, the corps of cadets of the Salvadoran military academy was transported to Fort Benning, Georgia, to undergo a version of the U.S. Army's Officer Candidate School conducted entirely in Spanish that emphasized the essentiality of observing human rights, of avoiding harm to non-combatants, and of wresting popular

---

17. *Discriminate Deterrence*. Report of the Commission on Integrated Long-Term Strategy, January 1988, 15-16. Group was convened toward the end of President Reagan's second term, and was co-chaired by Fred Iklé and Albert Wohlstetter.
18. Commander-in-Chief, U.S. Southern Command, as the responsible commander was then entitled.

support away from the guerrillas. This American Officer Candidate School created for the Salvadoran Army a cadre of junior officers significantly more effective in field operations, and more responsive to American advice. Equally important, the government of Honduras allowed entire units of the Salvadoran Army to enter their territory for the purpose of conducting counter-guerrilla field exercises under the tutelage of American Special Forces. Moreover, units of the U.S. National Guard were invited to conduct training exercises with Honduran troops: building roads and bridges, rectifying water supplies, and practicing medicine.[19] These drills in Honduras set new operational standards for Salvadoran and Honduran commanders.

In the foreseeable future, the need for understanding human dynamics will continue to be important as the United States interacts with numerous foreign cultures to achieve national security goals and objectives. U.S. military forces were largely unready for their post-September 11 missions, which reached beyond combat operations, to stability, reconstruction, and humanitarian responses—a result of little attention or investment in past decades to retain or improve the nation's military posture in these areas.

The Department must avoid loss of focus and needed human dynamics capabilities when current engagements subside. Human dynamics capabilities are not only important for future military engagements but are equally valuable in shaping events before hostilities are underway—perhaps even preventing hostilities. Today, the military departments have many efforts underway to increase the linguistic and cultural understanding of their forces, as will be discussed in more detail in later sections of this report. But these many activities are not well coordinated, nor is there effective department-wide leadership in this area.

---

19. A turning-point in the war, for there were many in Washington who believed that anti-Americanism in Honduras was so strong that Roberto Suazo Cordoba, President of the fledging democracy in Honduras, would be overturned; moreover, El Salvador and Honduras were long-time antagonists, at war with each other as recently as 1969. The president made a courageously bold decision in inviting foreign troops into his country. N.B. He agreed to an American presence only on the proviso that the first unit deployed would be a U.S. Army field hospital.

Findings

Human dynamics and cultural understanding will continue to be important in future military operations.

- Military training should persistently stress discretion in the use of force.

- Stability operations require human dynamics capabilities and can succeed only with close collaboration between the Departments of State and Defense and among related government agencies.

- Cultural insensitivity is militarily dysfunctional.

DoD and its components are funding different efforts to collect, analyze, and disseminate information related to human dynamics. However:

- These efforts are not effectively tied to an overarching formal or informal DoD requirement.

- The efforts often are duplicative

RECOMMENDATION #1. COORDINATION & LEADERSHIP

The Secretary of Defense should:

- **Instruct his staff to develop a comprehensive strategy** that builds upon programs now underway in the Army and Marine Corps to assure human dynamics awareness for future stability operations. This strategy should also include directives on education and training, human dynamics advisors, and knowledge management, as outlined below.

- Review and determine the best course of action to **establish effective oversight and coordination of human dynamic activities**.

- **Ensure that the implications for force structure and DoD appropriations** of all the recommendations of this report are considered in the upcoming Quadrennial Defense Review.

The Chairman of the Joint Chiefs should direct a regional combatant commander to develop tactics, techniques, and procedures for employing enhanced knowledge of human dynamics in anticipation of stability operations with U.S. forces in non-combatant roles, cooperating closely with other combatant commands, U.S. agencies, and non-government organizations (NGOs), as well as allies and host nations.

Chapter 4. Interagency and Civil Society Participation

> [Future military] challenges … cannot be overcome by military means alone and they extend well beyond the traditional domain of any single government agency or department. They require our government to operate with unity, agility and creativity, and will require devoting considerably more resources to non-military instruments of national power. [20]
>
> Secretary of Defense Robert M. Gates

Future expeditionary operations for the U.S. military will be complex and will increasingly require coordination and cooperation with multiple stakeholders in order to successfully accomplish a mission. Military power will need to be synchronized with diplomatic, economic, and information domain actions. Success will require more than effective joint operations among the military services—it will require coordination and collaboration outside DoD.

Organizing for Multi-stakeholder Collaboration

Effectively coordinating the capabilities of disparate organizations with conflicting procedures and competing priorities is a challenging task. But it is one that must be mastered if the United States is to achieve its national security objectives. As the nation increasingly seeks to use all diplomatic, informational, economic, and military instruments of national power, the U.S. military will be working in supported and supporting roles with other commands and agencies.

---

20. Speech at Center for Strategic and International Studies, January 26, 2008.

Non-governmental and Civil Society Organizations

A wide range of NGOs have broad capabilities, relationships, and local knowledge.

A wide range of NGOs have broad capabilities, relationships, and local knowledge. NGOs increasingly partner with businesses as well as with governments to achieve both local and global results.

In his October 2007 letter to the combatant commanders, Chairman of the Joint Chiefs Admiral Michael Mullen directed them to "build and reinvigorate relationships through Theater Security Cooperation with a focus on capacity-building, humanitarian assistance, regional frameworks for improving governance, and cooperation in enforcing the rule of law." To achieve this goal, men and women at all levels in the combatant commands will need to work increasingly with nongovernment organization (NGO) staff members in a spirit of cooperation and coordination rather than of command and control. Successful examples of cooperation include the following:

- U.S. Southern Command reorganization, that promotes joint, interagency and private- and public-sector cooperation[21]

---

21. The reorganization supports the concept that the military cannot tackle 21st-century security challenges alone. As described by Admiral James Stavridis, Commander of U.S. Southern Command, "We are working to create an organization that can best adapt itself to working with the interagency, with our international partners and even with the private-public sector. And we want to do it in a way that is completely supportive of all our partners... our objective is to become the best possible international, interagency partner we can be." http://www.southcom.mil/AppsSC/news.php?storyId=1323 [January 26, 2009]

- 2007 USNS *Comfort* Latin American Humanitarian Mission
- Tsunami relief effort utilizing U.S. military assets to provide transportation, logistics, and communications

A Whole-of-Government Approach

Since 2003, the U.S. Army has been conducting Unified Quest exercises on realistic threats to peace around the world. Unified Quest 2008 was conducted at the U.S. Army War College and co-sponsored by Joint Forces Command and Special Forces Command. Participants in the exercises include current and former military officers, as well as representatives from academia, industry, and other government agencies. These exercises continue to reinforce the lesson that the Army cannot solve every problem alone. Rather, it must work in concert with other agencies, departments, and foreign entities to deal with all facets of anticipated conflicts. The need for a "whole-of-government" approach has been repeatedly demonstrated through these exercises.

As explained by MG Barbara Fast: "One of the main ideas of the game (Unified Quest) is the concept of 'building partnership capacity' and understanding how the Army can better coordinate with other U.S. agencies and departments when responding to these unique future conflicts throughout the world. ... Much of what we're talking about, more than ever, requires a whole-of-government approach."[22]

> ... Much of what we're talking about, more than ever, requires a whole-of-government approach ... [working] in concert with other agencies, departments, and foreign entities to deal with all facets of anticipated conflicts.

Capacity Building and Civil-Military Operations

A number of DoD and other U.S. government-sponsored entities are devoted to capacity building and civil-military operations, including the following examples:

---

22. MG Barbara Fast, Deputy Director, Army Capabilities Integration Center, quoted in *Carlisle Barracks Banner*, May 2008.

- **Human Terrain Teams**. Developed by the U.S. Army to provide commanders with a better understanding of the people, customs, beliefs, and motivating factors of the populations among whom their U.S. military units are deployed. Teams, which are currently deployed in Afghanistan and Iraq, with both the Army and the Marine Corps, are designed to assist brigades and higher echelon units with social science research analysis and advice in the area of responsibility.

- **Provincial Reconstruction Teams**. Teams of experts designed to help local governments develop their capacity to govern, to promote economic development, and to increase security. The teams are embedded with U.S. brigades at a forward operating base, which provides logistical and security support. However, the teams are under direction of the Department of State Foreign Service Officer who heads them.

- **Africa Partnership Station**. A U.S.-led response to requests by African nations for military-to-military or civilian-military maritime training. This activity provides a platform to support sustained training and collaboration on a regional scale in West and Central Africa that will enhance situational awareness and improve control by the nations themselves over their maritime environment. Such cooperative partnerships seek to increase the professional capabilities and capacity of Africans on those security matters that are of most interest to them and that they themselves have identified.

Intellectual Capital

During the Second World War, DoD supported independent research centers, such as the Human Relations Area Files at Yale University, as available resources for in-depth investigations of human dynamics issues relevant to national security interests. During the Cold War, the U.S. Government sought to increase the nation's intellectual capital through creation of the National Defense Education Act. This act emphasized math, science, and engineering as disciplines essential to the perceived challenges of the adversaries of that time. DoD also created additional independent research centers, such as RAND, to serve the information needs of the U.S. military.

The human dynamics intellectual challenges associated with U.S. national security today are much broader than those of the Cold War and require deeper supporting knowledge and experience to inform the actions of members of the U.S. government at all levels. Globalized economics, commerce, trade, and humanitarian aid have also created new venues of intellectual capital that do not currently exist within the U.S. government. Academic, commercial, nongovernmental, and interagency environments are all communities of interest with which the U.S. military must be prepared to interact. Effort is needed now to expand the search for resources outside government that will engage these communities in future cooperative efforts.

Academic Curricula and Research

"Despite successes in the past and present, it is an unfortunate reality that many people believe there is this sharp divide between academia and the military—that each continues to look on the other with a jaundiced eye. These feelings are rooted in history—academics who felt used and disenchanted after Vietnam, and troops who felt abandoned and unfairly criticized by academia during the same time. And who often feel that academia today does not support them or their efforts."[23]

Such views will not serve the Department well in the future. DoD should engage with and draw on the expertise in academia to inform and enhance its human dynamics capabilities as well as to expand opportunities for training and education:

---

23. Secretary of Defense Robert M. Gates before the Association of American Universities (14 April 2008).

- **National Security Education Program**. This program sponsors graduate fellowships for students undertaking research and language acquisition in a variety of countries. The program also sponsors the Reserve Officer Training Corps (ROTC) Language and Culture Project, which provides opportunities to undergraduate ROTC cadets and midshipmen to study languages and cultures of increasing importance to U.S. national security, and prepares them for the global operations of the U.S. military.

- **DoD Regional Centers**. Regional cooperation, capacity building, and information sharing can be facilitated through positive and durable relations between military and civilian partners. The five DoD Regional Centers (Africa Center for Strategic Studies, Asia Pacific Center for Security Studies, Center for Hemispheric Defense Studies, George C. Marshall European Center for Security Studies, and Near East-South Asia Center for Strategic Studies) were established to support achievement of this goal.

- **Consortium for Complex Operations**. The Consortium for Complex Operations is a Department of Defense-led collaboration with the Department of State and United States Agency for International Development. The consortium supports separate but conceptually related Departments of Defense and State stability operations, counterinsurgency, and irregular warfare efforts—collectively called "complex operations." Principal roles of the consortium include serving as an information clearinghouse and cultivating a community of practice for complex operations training and education comprised of civilian and military educators, trainers, and lessons learned practitioners dedicated to improving U.S. preparation for complex operations.

- **Minerva Consortia**. Recently launched and funded through a memorandum of understanding between the Department of Defense and the National Science Foundation, this university consortia will promote research into specific areas in which the Department of Defense, and perhaps other government agencies, seeks to increase its depth of knowledge and explore alternative points of view. Participating academic institutions could also become repositories of open-source documentary archives to foster collaborative research. Four research areas are currently under investigation for potential sponsorship by DoD: Chinese military and technology studies, Iraqi and terrorist perspectives, religious and ideological studies, and new disciplines in social sciences.

Commercial

Private enterprise has developed considerable capacity for interfacing with cultures, sub-cultures, and audiences of all types. As a means of identifying opportunities for market expansion of commercial products and services, such knowledge is essential to global business management:

- **Global Marketplace Knowledge**. Global market research firms offer clients insight into the consumer behaviors of many countries. Extensive demographic, attitudinal, behavioral, product/service consumption, and media consumption information are just some of the data collected to facilitate identification of target consumers, evaluate potential new product opportunities, and reveal new marketing and communication strategies.

- **Global Public Opinion Polls**. Global public opinion polls seek to provide insight into the thoughts of the world's adult population on such issues as personal aspirations, well-being, healthcare, war and peace, employment, household income, and environmental trends. The Pew Global Attitudes Project and the Gallup World Poll are two prominent polling organizations that provide such insights.

Future Opportunities

One proposed new organization that could further the government's needs to expand its understanding of human dynamics is the **Center for Global Engagement**. Proposed by the Defense Science Board in 2007, this congressionally funded center would serve as a collaborative hub for U.S. government innovation in cultural understanding, communication technology, resource identification, and creative program development.[24] The center would engage experts, thought leaders, and creative talent from the private sector and civil society in support of U.S. strategic communication and public diplomacy.

Building New Relationships

While some social scientists are concerned about the ethical implications of cooperating with the national security community, this by no means indicates universal opposition. Even among critics of present government policy, dissatisfaction sometimes manifests itself as a desire to have more, not less, input into governmental affairs. It is also true that the relationship between physical scientists and the national security community has been closer and much better established than that between social scientists and DoD.[25]

However, the relationship between DoD and certain disciplines within the social science community has consistently been close and mutually beneficial. These successes suggest further prospects for cooperation that will serve both scholarship and national security needs:

---

24. *Report of the Defense Science Board Task Force on Strategic Communications,* January 2008.
25. For a popular history of one illustrative, if particularly important, aspect of that cooperation, see Ann Finkbeiner, *The Jasons: The Secret History of Science's Postwar Elite,* (New York: Penguin, 2006).

- One scholar describes the birth of interdisciplinary approaches to social science and certain area studies fields as a direct legacy of the collaboration established within the Research & Analysis Branch of the Office of Strategic Services during the Second World War.[26]

- Historians and political scientists are thoroughly interwoven into the national security community to the benefit of all sides. Among the prominent historians and political scientists who have served in the government, or defense think-tanks, or who have benefitted from access to records held by the U.S. government are Gerhard Weinberg, Gordon Craig, Carl Schorske, and Alexander George.[27]

- Scholar-practitioners who have worked in both academic social science and in government include Herbert Marcuse, Francis Fukuyama, Henry Kissinger, Zbigniew Brzezinski, Anthony Lake, and Zalmay Khalilzad.[28]

- There are general officers in the military who earned advanced degrees in history and other social sciences and who have taught in academia, such as General John R. Galvin, USA (Ret.); Major General Robert H. Scales, Jr., USA (Ret.); General David H. Petraeus, USA; and Lieutenant General William E. Odom, USA (Ret.).[29]

---

26. Barry Katz, *Foreign Intelligence: Research and Analysis in the Office of Strategic Services*, 1942-1945, (Cambridge: Harvard University Press, 1990).
27. Weinberg, William Rand Kenan, Jr. Professor of History, Emeritus, University of North Carolina at Chapel Hill; Craig, J. E. Wallace Sterling Professor of Humanities, Emeritus, Stanford University; Schorske, Dayton-Stockton Professor of History, Emeritus, Princeton University; George, Graham H. Stuart Professor of International Relations, Emeritus, Stanford University.
28. Herbert Marcuse, Office of Strategic Services and U.S. Department of State, Professor at Columbia, Harvard, and Brandise Universitites, and University of California at San Diego; Francis Fukuyama, Policy Planning Staff, U.S. Department of State, Professor at John Hopkins and George Mason Universities; Henry Kissinger, National Security Advisor and 56th Secretary of State, Professor at Harvard University; Zbigniew Brzezinski, National Security Advisor, Professor at Johns Hopkins University; Anthony Lake, National Security Advisor, Professor at Georgetow n University; Zalmay Khalilzad, Ambassador to Iraq and Afghanistan, associate professor at University of California at San Diego.
29. Prior to retiring, Galvin served as former Supreme Allied Commander, Europe, and Chief of the U.S. European Command; Scales retired from the Army as Commandant of the United

- Geographers make contributions to numerous aspects of the national security community. One member of the field has written that "World War II was the best thing that has happened to geography since the birth of Strabo [~63BC to 24AD]." In his estimate, the involvement of geographers in the war effort opened their field of view and made their work less small-scale and inwardly focused.[30] Though there was some discomfort at the secrecy involved, geographers were integral to the development of the American satellite reconnaissance program and subsequently reaped great benefits from the resulting methods and data.[31]

- Economists are thoroughly integrated into the national security community and played an instrumental role in the development of deterrence theory that helped keep the peace during the Cold War.[32] Among the Nobel Prize-winning economists who have worked at the RAND Corporation, for instance, are Thomas Schelling and Kenneth Arrow. The latter has written that "my work on social choice and on Pareto efficiency dated from this period [at RAND]."[33] Five presidents of the American Economic Association served in the Research and Analysis Branch of the Office of Strategic Services.

States Army War college; Odom served as Director, National Security Agency; and Petraeus serves as Commander, U.S. Central Command.

30. Kirk H. Stone, "Geography's Wartime Service," *Annals of the Association of American Geographers,* 69:1 (1979), pp. 89-96.

31. John Cloud, "Imaging the World in a Barrel: CORONA and the Clandestine Convergence of the Earth Sciences," *Social Studies of Science,* 31:2 (2001), pp. 231-251.

32. Fred Kaplan, *The Wizards of Armageddon,* (Stanford: Stanford University Press, 1991).

33. http://nobelprize.org/nobel_prizes/economics/laureates/1972/arrow -autobio.html, accessed June 25, 2008.

RECOMMENDATION #2. INTERAGENCY AND CIVIL SOCIETY PARTICIPATION

The Under Secretary of Defense for Policy should:

- **Expand Unified Quest 09 exercises** to include two additional teams: private sector and non-government humanitarian organizations.

- **Review commercial approaches to human dynamics information collection and analyses** to assess relevance to the U.S. government.

- **Fund and launch the Center for Global Engagement,** recommended in a prior DSB study, to provide a centralized U.S. government interagency center for human dynamics knowledge and surge capacity.

The Under Secretary of Defense for Personnel and Readiness should increase teamwork training for military members expected to work with NGO and private sector partners, emphasizing coordination and cooperation skills associated with those partnerships.

Chapter 5. Education, Training, and Expertise

All U.S. military services have undertaken efforts to increase cultural awareness among American forces during the last five years. However, none have been altogether successful in overcoming early setbacks in Iraq and Afghanistan due to adherence to accustomed methods and means, time urgencies of U.S. Central Command operations, the constraints imposed by authorized force structure, and domestic fiscal and political realities.

Education and training for cultural awareness, and improved training coordination within DoD are necessary, both to win the "war we are in" and to prepare for future operations.

In May 2008, Secretary of Defense Robert Gates was impelled to warn against succumbing to "next-war-itis"—the propensity of much of the defense establishment to favor programs aimed at what might be needed in a future conflict, as though to wish away the pressures that Operation Iraqi Freedom (OIF) and Operation Enduring Freedom (OEF) now exert upon the ground forces, especially the Army. Gates noted that, "The risk of over-extending the Army is real. But I believe the risk is far greater—to that institution, as well as to our country—if we were to fail in Iraq…That is the war we are in. That is the war we must win."[34]

In addition, the use of advisors to provide supplemental socio-cultural knowledge and insights provides numerous benefits to the operational military. Each of these elements is addressed in this chapter.

---

34. Reuters, 13 May 2008. "U.S. Must Focus On Iraq, Less On Future Wars: Gates"

Train for Cultural Awareness

Following the failure to reestablish stability after the "regime change" in Iraq,[35] the Services have undertaken to train forces in cultural awareness, develop advisory programs, and improve professional military education with the aim of improving the abilities of rank and file to plan for and conduct stability operations. Activities range from establishing appropriate doctrine through laudable initiatives by unit commanders (the Army and the Marine Corps collaborated on a joint manual on counterinsurgency),[36] reconfiguring large training facilities (such as the Army's facilities at Forts Irwin and Polk and the Marine Corps' at 29 Palms), and creating cultural simulations suitable for pre-deployment mission readiness exercises. Some of the broader service-specific efforts are described below.

U.S. Army

The U.S. Army recognizes that its units need to have an understanding of cultural factors and social norms, as well as linguistic proficiency in order to conduct full spectrum operations anywhere around the world (as described in its new FM 3-0).[37] This holds for operations being conducted in Iraq and Afghanistan today and, based on current projections, will likely be true in future operations. Programs and actions in the U.S. Army include the following:

- **A comprehensive strategy to develop**, as an Army core competency, **cultural and language skills** requisite for planning and conducting operations. The strategy has three overarching objectives: (1) units having cultural skills and foreign language capabilities for full spectrum operations; (2)

35. Interview with LtG Jay Garner. His plan was predicated on expected use by Saddam Hussein of WMD, and on employing the Iraqi Army for reconstruction. http://www.pbs.org/wgbh/pages/frontline/shows/truth/interviews/garner.html.
36. For example, techniques reported above by the 3rd ACR under Col. H.R. McMaster to exploit operationally the expertise of a historian, one of the U.S. Army's few Arabist Foreign Area Officers. Teleconference interview with Colonel H. R. McMaster, Daniel Barnard, and members of the DSB Task Force on Understanding Human Dynamics, November 27, 2007, Arlington, Virginia.
37. Except as otherwise noted, this section was derived from interviews at Headquarters, U.S. Army Training and Doctrine Command.

leaders possessing culture and foreign language competencies for U.S., allied, and coalition operations at any time; (3) soldiers with a balanced set of culture and foreign language competencies. The strategy incorporates culture and foreign language knowledge and understanding through professional military education and training for individual soldiers. It incorporates cultural and language enablers that are essential to the performance of military tasks in unit training programs as well as in preparation for deployment. It also provides brigade combat and regimental combat teams with relevant, socio-cultural information and knowledge, and dedicated expertise to integrate into their decision-making.

- **Home station training programs**, augmented by support from the Defense Language Institute and the U.S. Training and Doctrine Command (TRADOC) Cultural Center located at Fort Huachuca, have served to deepen understanding of culture and language as it pertains to current operations in Iraq and Afghanistan. TRADOC Cultural Center's mandate is to provide the U.S. Army with mission-focused culture education and training, whether in units or in TRADOC's schools and centers.

- **Provincial Reconstruction Teams** are structured and trained to assist a particular Iraqi or Afghan local government in providing basic services to its citizens. The Army has dedicated a prime unit of its active force structure, a line brigade combat team—1st BCT, 1st Infantry Division at Fort Riley, Kansas—to work with the teams and instill in their members that cultural awareness is requisite for subsequent service in the Iraq and Afghanistan theaters. These represent important progress toward developing capability to conduct stability operations. Provincial Reconstruction Teams have been welcomed in the field, but the undertaking is nascent, and the first teams have been judged by some as undermanned and less than cohesive.[38]

---

38. Cf. http://www.washingtonindependent.com/view/civilians-missing.

- The **Human Terrain System** (HTS), which includes forward deployed Human Terrain Teams, a Research Reachback Center for support to forward teams, a Subject Matter Expert Network for additional research and analysis, and the Mapping the Human Terrain Toolkit for archiving and visualization of socio-cultural information. **Human Terrain Teams** are trained and deployed for direct support at the brigade, division, and corps level. These teams collect and analyze socio-cultural information and assist commanders and staffs in using that information in their planning and decision-making. They also serve as "institutional memory" during unit rotations. Teams are currently deployed in Iraq and Afghanistan with all brigades, divisions, and corps. Success of these teams is tied to the focus on capability where it is most needed—at the tactical level where understanding and interaction with the local population really matters. Having teams at multiple echelons allows for aggregation of socio-cultural information, providing a common operating picture to units at all levels.

Human Terrain Teams, currently deployed in Iraq and Afghanistan, collect and analyze socio-cultural information.

U.S. Marine Corps

The U.S. Marine Corps has instituted, at Quantico, Virginia, the Center for Advanced Operational Culture Learning (CAOCL) with the following mission: "Ensure Marines are equipped with requisite regional, culture, and language knowledge to allow them to plan and operate successfully in the joint expeditionary environment in any region of the world in current and potential operating conditions, targeting persistent and emerging irregular, traditional, catastrophic and disruptive threats."[39]

The priorities of CAOCL's effort are as follows:

- Persistent home station and pre-deployment training for operational forces and The Marine Special Operations Advisor Group (MSOAG)

- Support to the schoolhouses and distance learning

- Scenario performance-based "elementary" language learning:
  - support for the operating forces/MSOAG/advisors
  - support sustainment language training

- Career Marine Regional Studies Program

To execute its mission, CAOCL launched the Career Marine Regional Studies Program—courses of instruction in 17 "micro-regions" of the world, including regions such as Transcaucasus, Central Asia, and the Balkans. All Marine officers and enlisted members after their second enlistment must meet specific learning objectives in at least one of these micro-regions. The program uses a mix of distance learning, schoolhouse courses, directed reading, and other instructional materials to provide every Marine operational culture and language learning.

---

39. Center for Advanced Operational Culture Learning, Briefing to the Defense Science Board Task Force on Understanding Hunan Dynamics, April 29, 2008.

U.S. Air Force

At the Air University (Maxwell-Gunter AFB, Montgomery, AL) the U.S. Air Force has established a broad program of education, research, and development on culture and language, directed from the following "centers."[40]

Cultural and Language Center. Formed in 2006, the Center supports the Expeditionary Air Force by providing airmen at all ranks with the best available understanding of foreign cultures and the competencies to communicate and collaborate effectively with members of foreign societies. The center conducts and sponsors research into the development of cross-cultural competencies by U.S. Air Force personnel, as well as research addressing the requirement for specific skills needed by individuals in particular assignments and roles. The Air Force vision for the center is that it will become a premier Department of Defense institution for defining cross-cultural competencies, developing conceptual tools to facilitate analysis of culturally distinct behavior, and sponsoring cutting-edge research into cross-cultural communications.

Behavioral Influences Analysis Center. Established in 2006, the center provides responsive, authoritative, reliable support to professional military education, operational level warfighters, and policy makers to enable understanding, holistic planning, and exploitation of the perceptual and behavioral dimensions of the "human terrain" of any military or military-supported mission. Its principal missions are curriculum design, adversary/other behavioral modeling, reach back analysis support, and red team and alternative/competitive analysis on motivations, intentions, and likely behaviors.

The center is professionally and procedurally advised and evaluated by a network of subject matter experts and practitioners in social, behavioral, cognitive, decision, and computational sciences. Specialists from the liberal arts, humanities, linguistics, and analysis disciplines are part of the center's "national advisory network." These experts and practitioners work and contribute within the national security,

---

40. http://www.au.af.mil/au/viewNews.asp?storyid=101

academic, intelligence, research, and science and technology domains. This network of experts will participate in a wide range of center activities—reviewing analyses and assessments; participating on red team development, training, and execution; and providing constructive inputs to the center's direction and activities.

The Behavioral Influences Analysis Center is expected to evolve into the center of excellence, and advisory activity of choice, for operational level warfighters in their student and practitioner roles.

Negotiation Center of Excellence. This center is the U.S. Air Force resource to prepare participants for negotiations in a wide range of circumstances: international, crisis, hostage, labor- and job-related, acquisition and contracts, environmental, alternative dispute resolution, consensus building, mediation, and facilitation.

Findings on Education, Training, and Expertise

- The armed services have programs underway to build cultural awareness for stability operations, to acquire germane data, and to use communication for training and consultation. However, these programs are disparate, with little evidence of coordination, either among the services, with a combatant command, or by the Office of the Secretary of Defense (OSD).

- The USMC's Career Marine Regional Studies program requires all officers and NCOs to demonstrate learning from material on the culture(s) of one of 17 regions worldwide. Unfortunately its distance learning technology is mundane, and, as a result, the program probably will have little impact on current conflicts. It may also invite criticism from OSD as "next-war-itis."

- The U.S. Air Force has positioned at the Air University a set of "centers" that could become useful in developing insights into foreign cultures for stability operations, but at present these appear to lack the tactical focus that ground forces require.

- The Army's programs are not yet closely coupled, but TRADOC is developing a holistic strategy that embraces cultural awareness and linguistic skills for operational readiness:

- Mission-readiness exercises at combat training centers surely assist in developing cultural awareness, but being of short duration, are of doubtful use for particular missions in a specific place overseas.

- Similarly, modification of professional military education courses to shoehorn time for generic cultural awareness into curricula can make only a modest contribution to any particular operation.

- Use of a prime combat force unit—such as 1st BCT, 1st ID—to prepare Provincial Reconstruction Teams must be viewed as an expedient, and should be replaced soon by other means and methods.

- The evolving Human Terrain System, which includes Human Terrain Teams, Research Reachback Center support, and ongoing knowledge base, seems likely to provide useful support to military units at all echelons, as well as to country teams and Provisional Reconstruction Teams engaged in all types of operations conducted among populations. The lessons learned from the OIF and OEF experiment with HTS is that baseline knowledge of the cultures and societies in areas where future operations might be conducted is more effective than developing critical capabilities and knowledge at the last minute. Such knowledge of human dynamics may also reduce the need for or scope of future military intervention. However, given that the HTS is currently a proof-of-concept and not yet a program of record, it is not clear whether resources, force structure, and funding will be available to institutionalize HTS so that it can be sized to match a combatant commander's force requirements and be integrated into the Army's plan for force generation and pre-deployment (derived from a model called ARFORGEN).

- Both Air Force and Army reportedly maintain extensive networks of consultants among social scientists.

Training Coordination

Several proposals have been advanced for establishing one or more new DoD institutions charged with overseeing all education, training, and operations within the Department that entail cultural expertise or social science in its numerous disciplines.[41] In one sense, this enthusiasm for the betterment of soldier pre-combat knowledge and discernment is encouraging to those familiar with the sketchy pamphlets provided soldiers prior to World War II invasions. The armed services share the perception that there is a need to improve their cultural awareness, but as Secretary Gates points out, they are at war. They have little time to engage in bureaucratic or legalistic battles to defend ameliorating concepts and existing organizations, however imperfect. Within DoD, current organizations exist in response to explicit requirements of the combatant command, and their existence is consistent with the intent of Congress, as the law regarding the Army indicates:[42]

TITLE 10--ARMED FORCES Subtitle B. Army
PART I. ORGANIZATION CHAPTER 307--THE ARMY
Sec. 3062. Policy; composition; organized
peace establishment

It is the intent of Congress to provide an Army that is capable, in conjunction with the other armed forces, of (1) preserving the peace and security, and providing for the defense, of the United States, the Commonwealths and possessions, and any areas occupied by the United States; (2) supporting the national policies; (3) implementing the national objectives; and (4) overcoming any nations responsible for aggressive acts that imperil the peace and security of the United States.

---

41. Such as Dr. John Chin's proposal for required pre-deployment training: "phased synchronized quality controlled cultural intelligence education" for all DoD personnel, and targeted and tailored add-on for specialists such as Provincial Reconstruction Teams and Human Terrain Teams members, all under a Single Cultural Intelligence Education Center and a Standing Cultural Education Advisory Group.
42. http://frwebgate.access.gpo.gov/cgibin/getdoc.cgi?dbname=brow se_usc&docid= Cite:+10USC3062>

The military services have undertaken efforts to increase cultural awareness among American forces

It is possible that OSD could obtain interagency agreement and congressional support for a training center focused on developing teams of government and non-government representatives as Provincial Reconstruction Teams, or any future equivalent. The present gap in capabilities for stability operations is government-wide, extending well beyond DoD. That gap is generated by time-distance and fiscal constraints: non-DoD entities are reluctant to devote personnel to participate in pre-deployment training with a military unit, and feel unable to deploy them as a military sub-unit into a conflicted area overseas; nor have they received congressional authorization or funds for such purposes. There is also a lack of teamwork by members of other departments and agencies with units of the armed services engaged in operations overseas.

Given this government-wide gap, rather than a DoD center, it would be preferable to establish an Institute for Public Administration Training, independent of the Department of Defense, with a faculty that included military experts, skilled engineers, public safety advisers, medics, and social scientists. An interagency aegis may catalyze better understanding and support in the government outside DoD, as well as among non-government organizations and the private sector.

This proposal was advanced to a former State Department senior advisor for Iraq transition who responded that other issues would have to be addressed before an institute would be practicable. One important matter is that of resources. If budgets reflect national priorities, then our operations in Iraq are exclusively a military operation and are generally perceived as such by the American public. So if we believe in a "whole-of-government" approach, then the resources have to be there or such an institute will not be successful.

Further, such an institute could be most effective if partnered with an existing university. The university could develop a core competency and curriculum in stability operations that military and civilian personnel could attend—expanding the pool of people with expertise that could be used in support of future operations. Association with a university also makes such a program more accessible to individuals in non-government organizations.

Training Americans for stability operations also appears to be amenable to adroit use of DoD information technology: cooperative development of an appropriate database and exploitation of advanced tools for inter-cultural collaboration.[43]

It is fortuitous that the Distributed Common Ground Station (DCGS) is now approaching maturity. DCGS could organize, store, and distribute "human terrain information," provide tools to keep that data current, and continuously provide cultural insights from competent social scientists to analysts and operators alike. But there are significant issues of security classification and semantics to be resolved, among them means to communicate information to Americans without security clearances, or to their foreign counterparts.

Fortunately too, in November 2007 the Defense Information System Agency (DISA) commenced early user testing with Defense Connect Online (DCO),[44] a new component of collaboration tools for its Net-Centric Enterprise Services, providing capabilities for interactive chat and audio-visual multicasting across either its Secret Internet Protocol Router Network (SIPRNet), or its Unclassified but Sensitive Internet Protocol Router Network (NIPRNet). DCO embodies two commercial software applications—Adobe Connect web conferencing,

---

43. For example, Information Processing Technology Office in the Defense Advanced Research Projects Agency (DARPA) has made impressive progress toward automated translation of both spoken and written foreign languages in its programs TRANSTAC and GALE. Also, the Navy's Coalition Chat Program has resulted in the deployment of multilingual chat to enable real-time communication among coalition troops and with local populations.
44. https://www.dco.dod.mil

and Jabber instant messaging—and permits archiving and transmittal of graphics such as PowerPoint presentations to convey graphs, maps, diagrams, and photographs as well as text.

It is germane that a survey last autumn of software being used in U.S. ground force command posts in Iraq reported that Adobe Connect was in all command posts visited as a favored means of communicating over NIPRNet with Iraqi military and police.[45] Reportedly, Connect has proved to be an important means for information exchange between a Provincial Reconstruction Team and U.S. military command posts because the team itself is denied use of SIPRNet. Defense Connect Online was scheduled to enter a phase of Limited Operational Capability in spring 2008. DISA officials believe that it will be able to link transoceanic as well as transcontinental users.

During its early user testing, DCO has functioned reliably over transcontinental networks, and shown it has potential to interface gracefully with commercial sites such as iTunes University and Beyond Campus for disseminating multimedia educational materials to Internet users of laptops and iPods—chart presentations, videos, podcasts, and screencasts. In March 2008, the George C. Marshall Foundation, in conjunction with DISA's Office of GIG Enterprise Services and TRADOC's Army Training Support Center, conducted experiments at Duke University using DCO for guided experiential learning: two virtual staff rides of a battlefield remote in time and space (Cantigny, France, May 28 1918). In these trials a professional historian skilled with staff rides, from his home office in Northern Virginia, guided ROTC cadets at Duke (one group of seniors, the other of sophomores) through a PowerPoint-based learning experience using Socratic tutoring and role-playing. Post-virtual staff ride evaluations conducted by the Professor of Military Science showed that the cadets (learners):

- readily accepted the remote mentor, endorsed DCO technology, and interacted well with the mentor and with each other

---

45. Conducted by MITRE (Mr. Pitsko); undassified charts re: CPs at Arifjan, VBC, Speicher, Taji, Ballad, and Bagram.

- rated the virtual staff rides as better organized and presented than any other history instruction they had received at the university

- agreed strongly that the above tools improved their understanding of leadership in mid-intensity combat

Moreover, the mentor reported that he enjoyed his teaching experience, and urged its proliferation. Information technicians from Duke University and DISA engineers who monitored the events were in agreement that DCO showed unique potential for distance learning.

DCO's web-based interactivity also appears to offer an excellent way to develop lingual proficiency and cultural awareness. The Duke experiments demonstrated that DCO provides a distance learning capability that could enable a qualified expert—historian, anthropologist, sociologist, linguist—to teach officers or NCOs, or representatives of other government agencies or NGOs, aspects of foreign culture, including language skills, in a mode that facilitates discussion between expert and learners, and collaborative learning among all participants. Moreover, for such purposes, DCO could readily exploit current cultural-rich imagery such as that being collected in the Tactical Ground Reporting (TIGR) database.[46]

Additionally, using DCO for web conferencing would enable any governmental official or NGO representative, to participate from an office or home computer in military exercises or actual operations without the expense, travel time, and risks entailed in being on the scene.

---

46. A DARPA program being developed in Iraq, TIGR is a multimedia reporting system for soldiers at the patrol level, allowing users to collect and share information to improve situational awareness, and to facilitate collaboration and information analysis among junior officers. With its geo-spatial user interface, TIGR is particularly suited to counterinsurgency operations and enables collection and dissemination of fine-grained intelligence on people, places, and insurgent activity. Being focused on users at Company level and below, TIGR complements existing reporting systems that focus on the needs of users at Battalion or Brigade level and above.

Findings on Training Coordination

- Establishing an interagency training center for preparing teams of government and NGO representatives for stability operations, such as Provincial Reconstruction Teams, should prove to be very useful. It should, for example, foster interagency and NGO cooperation and enable the Army to return 1st BCT, 1ˢᵗ ID to operational use.

- DoD should engender interagency and congressional support for an Institute for Public Administration Training, possibly associated with a university, to (1) train American teams for aiding civic reconstruction and (2) for funding not only their training in the United States, but also their operations abroad.

- The Distributed Common Ground Station should host the cultural database for all DoD, but standards and means will have to be developed to govern data entry, search, retrieval and dissemination outside DoD.

- DISA's Defense Connect Online can support training for and conduct of stability operations. DCO can also support participation in training and operations through web-conferencing for non-DoD officials and NGO representatives.

RECOMMENDATION #3. EDUCATION AND TRAINING

The Secretary of Defense should instruct his staff to undertake the following:

- **Initiate interdepartmental action** to establish, with congressional support, an **Institute for Public Administration Training** with a faculty of military experts, skilled engineers, public safety advisors, medics, social scientists, and NGO representatives, tasked (1) to assist the Services and civil participants with readiness for catastrophe relief and stability operations, and (2) to form and train multi-disciplinary teams for augmentation of any U.S. country team.

- Invite participation of interagency and NGO representatives in **mission readiness exercises**, at least by telephone consultation during planning and in after-action review.

- Direct the Defense Information Systems Agency to bring to bear **a comprehensive set of collaborative services** that facilitate expert discovery, cross-domain security, and community creation to advance the human dynamics capabilities and cultural awareness efforts of the armed services and of the Institute for Public Administration Training.

- Support the Services in modifying the standard curriculum at U.S. military academies as well as service-specific curricula, to incorporate **basic training in human dynamics**.

RECOMMENDATION #4 HUMAN DYNAMICS ADVISORS

The Chairman, Joint Chiefs of Staff and the Under Secretary of Defense for Personnel and Readiness, with advice from the combatant commands, should direct increases in the "cultural bench" by factors of three to five:

- Expand curriculum in this area for **professional military education.**

- Improve **career paths** for human dynamics advisors.

- Provide relevant **advanced degree education**.

- Develop innovative processes for **recruiting and rewarding** human dynamic expertise.

- Increase the number of **Foreign Area Officers** and assign them more effectively.

- Establish **medium- and long-term requirements** for each combatant command.

USD (P&R) should work with the Services and combatant commands to combine and augment the separate pools of available consultants that are experts in particular cultures. The Assistant Secretary of Defense for Networks and Information Integration (ASD (NII)) should facilitate their connectivity and collaboration, both among themselves and with users.

Chapter 6. Science and Technology Programs and Investments

Technologies to support an understanding of human dynamics lie at the intersection of a broad set of disciplines: the social sciences (anthropology, psychology, sociology, political science, history, and economics), the biological sciences (neurobiology), and the mathematical sciences (computer science, graph theory, statistics, and mathematics). These typically independent disciplines have distinct histories, terminologies, methodologies (observational versus experimental) and evaluation approaches (quantitative versus qualitative), which sometimes lead to inconsistent practices, outcomes, and/or recommendations.

Bridging these divides, advancing interdisciplinary knowledge, and applying this collective knowledge to operational missions is essential to success. Notably, understanding human dynamics requires scarce cross-boundary knowledge, skills, and leadership. This situation is exacerbated by very rudimentary understanding of user requirements and primitive systems for human dynamics in relation to military operations.

Human and cultural studies include individual and group studies, cross-culturally and longitudinally, in the wide range of disciplines described above. But as has been discussed in previous chapters, there is no comprehensive, "one-stop entre" to, or compendium of, the findings, data, theories, models, and experts of relevance. Without a coordinating entity, it is difficult to catalog current investments, identify where future investments are needed, and even redirect investments as capabilities mature. Thus, to gain some understanding of the current investment landscape, the task force identified a broad, though not exhaustive, set of programs and investments.[47]

---

47. Responses to data call in Appendix D, ODDR&E overview of related efforts, and briefings on several preliminary DARPA efforts.

Based on this partial inventory of programs and investments, the task force concluded that current science and technology (S&T) activities can be divided into four categories: (1) language, (2) socio-cultural, (3) dynamic social network analysis, and (4) human dynamics computational modeling and simulation. Cross-cutting these four categories are research programs in areas such as individual behavior; group behavior; cognitive and neuro-processes; and social, economic, historical, and cultural processes.

As an illustration of the type of investment analysis needed in the area of human dynamics, task force members considered S&T investments in these four categories and performed a preliminary gap analysis, the highlights of which are shown in Table 1. This analysis began with assumed military requirements for human dynamics, identified what human dynamics capabilities are currently on hand or in development, compared the two to determine current gaps or shortfalls, and identified the associated S&T investment required to fill this gap. Gap analysis can be valuable for identifying S&T investment needs to support investment portfolio management.

In performing this preliminary analysis, it was noted that in the area of dynamic network analysis and social networks, numerous tools are currently available and new efforts in this area are not needed. These tools are mature, ready to be integrated with other technologies, and expanded, particularly for use in the areas of spatio-temporal reasoning and individual neuro-cognitive assessment.

Example Programs

In addition to the gap analysis conducted by members of the task force, the group heard briefings on a few ongoing S&T or S&T–related programs that provide examples of the type of current investments in the area of understanding human dynamics. Of the briefings the task force heard, the ones by the Defense Advanced Research Projects Agency (DARPA) comprised a small portfolio and those are outlined below as an example of current efforts.

Table 1. Human Dynamics Gap Analysis

Needs	Current Capability	Gap
Language (human language acquisition, automated translation and cultural factors)		
• Interagency Language Roundtable Read/Listen/Speak Level of 1+ C/S/A-wide and Level 3 in key C/S/A positions • Portable real time spoken language translation in hundreds of dialects • Rapid culture skill acquisition	• Variable language coverage (e.g., Europe good, Africa poor) • Text translation in major languages • Limited spoken language translation • Poor human and machine coverage of low-density languages • Difficult to define/project future language/dialect requirements	• Machine translation for low-density languages using limited training data • Machine transcription for multi-lingual audio • Multi-domain, multi-speaker spoken conversation transcription and translation • Intelligent, adaptive, immersive distributed language/culture learning environments • Track/promote language/culture skills
Human and Cultural Studies (psychological, sociological, cultural, economic, historic, neuro-cognitive, belief, and perception)		
• Worldwide, high fidelity data at the individual and group level (e.g., emotional response, belief systems, demographics, repeatable behavioral dynamics) • Semi-continuous updates of human/group/cultural data • Stakeholder analysis • Understanding and influence of recruitment, radicalization, and extremism • Portable, accurate deception detection • Understand how to use neuro, social, cultural and network information to strategically influence individual and group beliefs, values and behaviors	• Limited global demographic, attitude, and behavior data (e.g., country level polls) • Periodic, irregular data collection • Manual analyses • Culturally expert informants • Task specific neuro-cognitive and social-psychology studies • Limited use of human and cultural findings and technologies in field applications for rapid strategic influencing and in-field data collection of individual and group behavioral responses • Rapid cognitive-behavioral analysis (beyond decision-making) • Rapid cultural-assessment	• Broad and deep human and socio-cultural behavioral data sets • Advanced socio-cultural behavioral analytic tools (e.g., geo-statistical, psychographic, cognitive-social network, temporal and spatial visualization) • Automated ontology creation and revision tools • Automated assessment of the human terrain with emphasis on attitudes, influence networks and the effects of strategic communication • Lack maintained/federated databases with technologies for extracting knowledge from databases in a way that can be used to inform and validate dynamic network models • Automated sentiment/bias/intention/deception detection • Enhanced skills and technologies for ethnographic retrieval, rapid cultural assessments, rapid cognitive assessments, rapid rapport and in influencing • Gaming for virtual training and mission rehearsal

Table 1. Human Dynamics Gap Analysis (continued)

Needs	Current Capability	Gap
Dynamic Network Analysis		
• High fidelity, global social/behavioral/cognitive influence and transmission networks (and hidden networks) • Cross boundary network detection and tracking • Tactical and strategic reasoning using dynamic networks • Enhanced military dynamic network analysis training	• Basic social/behavioral/cognitive (strategic) influence, informationand disease transmission modeling • Manual and semi-automated influence and transmission network intelligence • Limited network evolution and what-if capability for course of action analysis • Tactical/operational/strategic network analysis tools, metrics, and models	• Complex, cross-boundary social network analysis • Automated meta-network detection and tracking from live data feeds, ethnographic data, text, and humint data • Statistical models for and procedures to estimate robustness of metrics on non-random networks • Spatio-temporal dynamic network analysis • Linking cognitive-neuro and dynamic network models to enable improved understanding of influence • Simulations driven from dynamic network data • Track/invest in dynamic network analysis skills
Modeling and Simulation (M&S)		
• Realistic, fine grained, multi level M&S—neuro to individual to group to society to global • M&S full spectrum of military and security operations • Forecasting aids for intelligence, influence operations, and planning	• Generic simulation engines • Limited real-time analysis • Limited tool interoperability • No common ontology • Retrospective modeling • Dated M&S military training	• Reusable models and simulations driven from captured operational data; accessible data • Open architecture platform for interoperability • Prediction of adversary (re)actions • Ethnographic and historical model calibration and/or validation • Translational research • New science of validation and analysis for human dynamics models and simulations • Track/invest in human dynamics modeling skills

Computational Social Science Portfolio. This DARPA portfolio comprises a number of preliminary investigative efforts.[48]

- **Integrated Crisis Early Warning System**, launched in October 2007, provides combatant commanders with a capability to proactively manage and respond to security risks in their area of operations—spanning the entire spectrum of the crisis early warning and mitigation cycle. The system integrates social science models, theories, and data across multiple levels of analysis to systematically identify antecedents to a variety of destabilizing events.

- **Technologies for Applications of Social Computing** is designed to create a social computing system that marries social theory, data, and methods. The system is intended to addresses questions at the tactical, operational, and strategic levels by developing reliable social simulation technologies to monitor, assess, and forecast the effects of events and courses of action on population segments—groups, leaders, and government institutions. The concept is to provide information that supports reliable, real-world decisions. In essence, the system will offer a TIVO-like capability for intelligence analysis and military operations that will provide a window on a world that cannot be viewed through traditional intelligence methods.

- **Strategic Communication Assessment and Analysis System** will be fed by two small, supporting investigations— automated sentiment analysis and disparate information networks—to devise an information planning and assessment capability. The objective of the effort underway is to evaluate the current state of technology against a use case to determine the analytic value of segmented network analyses and to address the potential analytic gains of fusing the various network technologies.

---

48. Sean O'Brien, "DARPA's Computational Social Science Portfolio," Briefing to the DSB Understanding Human Dynamics Task Force, June 4, 2008.

- **Conflict Modeling, Planning and Outcome Experimentation Program** provides a family of tools that will allow staffs to explore sources of instability and centers of power in a conflict environment, visualize and manage a comprehensive campaign plan, and explore multiple courses of action in different environments to see the range of outcomes.

The Potential of Neuroscience. DARPA is also exploring the potential of neuroscience research and development and its applications to understanding human dynamics. Advances in using neuroscience to understand the basis for human cognition, including non-invasive sensor technologies, may be applicable for understanding perception, the neurological origins of trust and compliance, and the neuroscience of persuasion—all relevant to the topic addressed in this report. The broad concept is to develop quantitative neuroscience tools and techniques to predict the effects of "ideas" within diverse populations. These concepts are the focus of a number of preliminary investigations.

Scientific understanding of the linkages among neuroscience, psycho-pharmacology, and cognition is important. Given new investigative tools (*e.g.*, fMRI, PET scans, brain implants, bioinformatics) worldwide knowledge will evolve rapidly in these areas. The JASON's study on human performance, urged the U.S. government to invest to stay ahead of adversary exploitation of this emerging knowledge.[49] Finally, the United States should monitor advances in brain-computer interfaces such as the use of external EEGs or neural implants to address severe disabilities or provide specialized sensory or mechanical output.

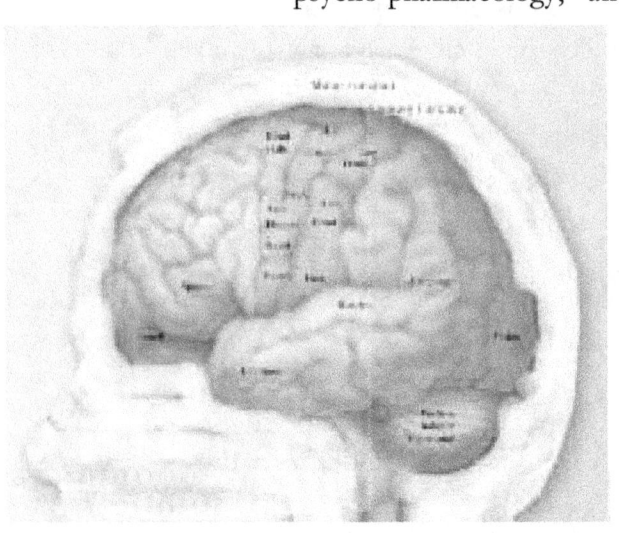

.... **exploring the potential of neuroscience research and development and its applications to understanding human dynamics.**

49. Williams, E. *et al*. JASON Report on Human Performance, JSR-07-625, March 2008.

Findings on S&T Programs and Investment

Based on its review of S&T programs and investment and the associated gap analysis, the task force made the following observations:

- Relevant investment in related S&T proved difficult to quantify. There is no common way of describing investments in this area and no comprehensive investment list. Furthermore, major efforts are funded by sources other than S&T, such as operational and maintenance accounts. Other efforts are add-ons to technology investments under the guise of S&T to support related training or human-computer interaction initiatives.

- Current investments appear to fall principally in four areas: (1) language, (2) socio-cultural, (3) dynamic social network analysis, and (4) human dynamics computational modeling and simulation.

- The technologies and scientific infrastructure for language and dynamic social network analysis have the highest level of maturity.

- Social network analysis and dynamic network analysis tools are mature, in use, and do not need to be reinvented. In addition, dynamic social network metrics (including centralities, exclusivities, and role-based metrics of leadership and power) have been validated, documented, and generally scale well. The key limitation is training on current tools and linking network-type reasoning to other areas. Two integrated areas of high promise are geo-spatial dynamic network analysis and the combination of neuro-cognitive models and dynamic network analysis in the area of influence, attitudes, and beliefs.

- Human and cultural studies and human dynamics computational modeling and simulation tools are less developed.

- While many tools are available, empirical socio-cultural data to populate these tools is often lacking.

- Comprehensive lists of such tools, models, data, and recognized experts are needed. Efforts to develop such lists have failed due to insufficient time and funding for such review activity and a lack of procedures and incentives for submitting information on new tools, models, and data.

RECOMMENDATION #5. SCIENCE & TECHNOLOGY INVESTMENTS

In the area of science and technology program investments, the task force recommends the following:

- DDR&E should establish a "portfolio manager" in human dynamics covering areas such as language, socio-cultural, dynamic network analysis, and human dynamics computational modeling and simulation to track tools, models, data, and experts. The responsibilities of the portfolio manager should include the following:

  - Define and develop a road map based on a refined gap analysis, coordinated with users—combatant commands and services. This roadmap should include a credible S&T budget and program.

  - DDR&E should review ongoing S&T programs (regardless of their budget authorities) in this area, in depth, and assess the potential based on data.

  - Define and implement a more robust research effort to explore the potential of relevant S&T efforts in cross-cutting human dynamics research linking dynamic network analysis to findings and models with direct military relevance.

Chapter 7. Human Dynamics Databases, Tools, and Products

Military operations conducted among populations present special challenges for assessing, reasoning about, and modeling human dynamics. Challenges include the need to rapidly shift to new regions of interest; the need to integrate and use data at varying levels of classification, owned by diverse parties, and collected for diverse needs; and the dynamic nature of human data due to the rapidly evolving set of actors, as well as changing lines of communication, allegiance, attitudes and beliefs among actors. The lines between enemies, adversaries, competitors, neutrals, and friends are blurred and make human dynamics astuteness essential.

Personnel at many echelons will need to flexibly respond and adapt to this fluid operational environment. They will need real-time access to expert knowledge sources as well as up-to-date accurate information on human dynamics. Such data include information on the social structure of various societies, formal and informal political systems, opinion leaders and political/military elite; who and what they influence and are influenced by; drug, gang, insurgent and terror organizations; norms, beliefs, and values; culturally specific manifestations of emotions; local traditions; needs and resources; and so on. They also need human dynamic models and simulations to support course of action analysis and planning.

> **The lines between enemies, adversaries, competitors, neutrals, and friends are blurred and make human dynamics astuteness essential. Personnel at many echelons will need to flexibly respond and adapt to this fluid operational environment. They will need real-time access to expert knowledge sources ... up-to-date accurate information on human dynamics ... human dynamic models and simulations to support ... analysis and planning**

Human dynamics awareness and situational understanding are essential to the planning and execution of military operations and will require increasing levels of granularity and data timeliness. DoD centers of excellence will need to be coordinated to ensure both breadth and depth of knowledge, as well as enhanced capability to adapt to emerging human dynamics challenges. Operations and reach-back cells will need to coordinate their efforts in order to ensure accurate and complete data, timely assessments, and detailed insight into the human terrain.

Given the importance of data, tools, and products in human dynamics, the task force paid considerable attention to these areas. As various programs were reviewed, model and simulation developers all expressed concern that they spent as much or more time collecting, fusing, and vetting data to initialize or validate their model as they did building the model and analyzing results. What data that did exist tended not to be shared or was too costly (as in data collected by nongovernment organizations such as Gallup), so that commonly available information, such as the Human Relations Area File, tended to be incomplete, out of date, and not in a form that can be used by models. Also, the necessary data often existed at a level of classification that limited its use. In addition, data providers and collectors were re-inventing models and simulations rather than providing data; but those models tended not to be well grounded in theory. The lack of common, shareable, maintained, and accurate data has limited the development of theory, re-usable models and simulations, and actionable intelligence for human dynamics.

A large number of human dynamics databases exist, but they are independent of each other, created for a specific element of the community, and do not effectively support users. These databases lack common formats, metadata or a unified ontology, and access is generally limited. Further, the majority of these databases are not maintained, fully populated, or interoperable. This is true at all levels from the neuro-cognitive to the socio-cultural. In addition, the task force found that although there is and has been significant investment in data collection, and although a great deal of data existed, discovery of and access to the appropriate data to meet user needs in a timely fashion was extremely difficult. This difficulty is due to the lack of a compendium describing available information, lack of data fusion facilities, inconsistent archiving, inability to easily search and retrieve data due to diverse architectures, and the fact that much data existed only in non-digital form.

Making relevant data available through a collaborative test bed with integrated use management to track the links between data, models, and experts will in the long run be more sustainable and better meet continuing DoD needs. This collaborative test bed needs to be flexible enough to support emergent technologies; have appropriate levels of access for cleanly moving tools, models, and simulations for use with data at different levels of classification; support search, storage, data fusion, and visualization; and leverage community involvement for data maintenance and tool, model, and simulation incorporation. The Intelligence Advanced Research Projects Activity's Research and Development Experimental Collaboration (RDEC) program and A-Space were movements in this direction but are not sufficiently open at the unclassified level and do not include community data contribution or maintenance.[50] Open, sharable models are an important trend. For example, the National Intelligence Council's 2020 Project Mapping the Global Future[51] actually published their models of "International Futures" on the web for others to reproduce results and support subsequent experimentation. The models capture economic, energy, agricultural, socio-political, and environmental subsystems for 182 countries interacting in a global system.

Another mission-critical area that would require a larger investment and have a longer time horizon is the area of "beliefs," encompassing attitudes, opinion trends, beliefs, and behaviors. In this case, there is less publically and militarily available data; the models and simulation are at a lower level of technical readiness; the tools for extracting the data less understood; and much of this is either "owned" and collected only on demand by private companies, is produced from polls, or must be extracted from texts and videos.

---

50. A-Space is a project of the Office of the Director of National Intelligence to develop a common collaborative workspace for all analysts within the Intelligence Community. Accessible from common workstations, the aim of the project is to provide access to interagency databases, a capability to search classified sources and the Internet simultaneously, web-based e-mail, and other collaboration tools. The RDEC program also involves the development of enhanced information sharing capabilities.
51. www.dni.gov/nic/NIC_2020_project.html

The Distributed Common Ground Station (DCGS)[52] has the capability to host the human and cultural database for all DoD. Standards and means need to be developed rapidly and disseminated widely to govern data entry, search, retrieval, and dissemination outside DoD and to encourage data entry and search by non-DoD researchers who support and enhance the DoD mission. Developing a tiered system with levels of access to different kinds of data would enable continued support for developing metrics, tools, products, models, and simulations at the unclassified level and supporting additional products at other levels of classification. New technologies, such as automated sentiment analysis, promise the ability to measure individual and group opinions and biases.

Barriers to Leveraging Existing Databases, Tools, Models, and Simulations

A number of barriers limit the U.S. military's ability to make sustained use of the best products, tools, models and simulations, and subject matter experts in the human dynamics area. As the tools and databases themselves are improved, the Department must address these barriers to gain maximum benefit from these various capabilities.

Understanding needs of the operator. Many developers of models and simulations have very limited understanding of military needs, and contracting officers often are not able to express them adequately. As a result, a large set of models are developed with little insight into actual operations.

Technology training. Additional technical training for military personnel and their advisors in the area of human dynamics would facilitate more effective use of current technology and products. Such training would help to enhance awareness of relevant experts and DoD-developed tools and models. In general, more training is needed at the undergraduate and graduate level in these militarily relevant human dynamics technologies.

---

52. The DCGS is a command and control system that is used throughout the ground forces and incorporates the Command Post of the Future. It is an ideal platform to host cultural databases and make them available to the users that need them.

Transitional research is needed to move tools, products, models, and simulations from proof-of-concept to operational use. It can dramatically reduce the time, costs, and other risks for this transition. This effort requires emphasis on re-use of tools and models in new situations, extensions of existing tools and models, development of user bases and training materials, replications of simulation experiments, lab experiments and field studies, development and maintenance of databases that support model development, testing and validation, and support for initial developers to engage in transition research.

Expertise. Much of the expertise in the area of human dynamics lies in academia and the businesses community. The ability to access this expertise is hindered by lack of a maintained database of human dynamics experts, both corporate and academic; differences in organizational culture; funding streams; and accreditation procedures. DoD can take steps to improve access by establishing and maintaining a single "rolodex" of subject matter experts, automating it through the deployment of expert locator tools, establishing procedures to better leverage these experts, and improving training in relevant disciplines for program managers. This is a key aspect of the proposed interagency Center for Global Engagement.

Interoperability and integration among databases, tools, and models is important. The current approach to engineering an enterprise-level system tends to focus on creating common data standards and interfaces, fixed ontologies, and common source code. However, such an approach is not sufficiently flexible to meet DoD needs, nor will it support the rapidly evolving nature of human dynamics data, theory, and methods. Instead, a service-oriented, open-type architecture is needed—one that supports evolving community standards, emergent ontologies, and facilitates use of proprietary models in association with test bed facilities and other environments. In conjunction, common metrics to test the validity of various tools, models, and simulations would be useful. Metrics need to be developed that are tailored for social/behavioral analysis, model calibration, and validation rather than simply applying existing scientific and engineering methods.

Findings on Databases, Tools, and Products

- While some data on human dynamics exist, they do not support model development testing and validation. The existing data are disorganized, out-of-date, not-comprehensive, not searchable, and, in many cases, on paper. In addition, the infrastructure to support gathering, distributing, and maintaining data is currently lacking.

- Little empirical socio-cultural data exist at the required granularity to support the military's operational and tactical missions. This has been true in prior conflicts, and is the case in both Iraq and Afghanistan.

- Non DoD involvement is critical to support the requisite level of model validation needed by DoD.

- Nongovernment organizations and subject matter experts can provide time-critical information needed by the military to support operations.

- There is little DoD understanding about how to appropriately use and validate human dynamics computational models and simulations. Further, there are no standards for methods or metrics for validation.

- At present, insufficient methods and resources are being applied to transition human dynamics technologies and models to operations.

RECOMMENDATION #6. DATABASES, TOOLS, PRODUCTS

In the area of data collection and analysis:

The Secretary of Defense should direct his staff to ensure interoperable databases. Actions should include:

- Review current and historic human dynamics data collection and database efforts for the extent to which they meet military need at the tactical, operational, and strategic levels.

- Design a suitable, distributed enterprise architecture, to allow user-friendly and rapid access to all databases, including the ability to share data among various databases in response to user queries, as appropriate.

- Promulgate standards for formats, evolving ontology, update schedules and processes, and maintenance procedures.

- Enforce these standards and promote buy-in from the community stakeholders inside and outside of DoD.

ASD (NII) should consolidate the databases germane to foreign culture and other human-dynamics-relevant areas into the Distributed Common Ground Station with appropriate provisions for collection, storage, retrieval, and dissemination at several levels of security.

The Under Secretary of Defense for Policy and the Under Secretary of Defense for Intelligence should increase efforts to collect human dynamics data and prepare these products so that information can be made available to multiple users. Actively engage departments and agencies government-wide as well as commercial and NGO resources and capabilities in collection and use of data and preparation of products.

The Under Secretary of Defense for Personnel and Readiness should ensure that there is a sufficient cadre of individuals with human dynamics astuteness to interpret the data and products.

Combatant commanders should direct population of these databases with regional information, generating requirements for both data collection and product preparation and evaluation. They should provide guidance, support, and resources (*e.g.* expertise and data collection technology) to forces deployed in their areas for documentation of short-term history.

Chapter 8. Summary and Final Thoughts

The detailed findings and recommendations summarized at the end of each chapter and in the executive summary will not be repeated again in this closing chapter. Instead, the paragraphs below are intended to briefly state the broad themes believed most appropriate for action under each topic and identify the highest priority recommendations.

As stated at the outset of this report, all military operations have a human dimension, yet this fact is often under-appreciated. History shows that human dynamics and culture have long shaped military conflicts—the Philippine and Vietnam Wars are two of many such examples. And in such circumstances, the United States has invested in understanding the human dimension, although often times it has done so belatedly. This has been true in recent years, when interventions in Afghanistan and Iraq once again returned the issue of human dynamics and culture to prominence.

What is being learned and the investments that are being made in response to current conflicts must not be lost, as has often happened in the past. Rather, an enduring capability is needed for the long term—one that extends beyond the focus of current military operations and institutionalizes human dynamics considerations into strategy, planning, doctrine, and training.

Understanding human dynamics is an essential ingredient to success across the full spectrum of military operations. What is being learned and the investments that are being made in response to current conflicts must not be lost, as has often happened in the past. Rather, an enduring capability is needed for the long term—one that extends beyond the focus of current military operations and institutionalizes human dynamics considerations into strategy, planning, doctrine, and training. In the judgment of the task force, improvements are needed to develop such a capability. Six areas have been discussed in the previous chapters and are highlighted here in summary.

Coordination and leadership. While many programs related to human dynamics understanding are underway in DoD, the task force found little evidence of coordination or of a comprehensive strategy. Such leadership activity is needed to ensure that current and future investments are made wisely, that the results of efforts across the Department are shared, and that focus on this important area is not lost once again. Further, development of a strategy has implications for force structure, training, and education.

Interagency and civil interactions. Organizations beyond DoD have expertise and experience in human dynamics—academia, nongovernment organizations, commercial industry, and other government organizations. Partnerships with such organizations are essential and must be developed and nurtured in order to achieve shared goals.

Education, training, and career development. The U.S. military services have already taken steps to expand the human dynamics content of education and training curricula. Such activities must endure and should be supported. In addition, development of an interagency training center, where government and nongovernment personnel can be trained together in multi-disciplinary teams, would have great value and support the type of future interagency participation required.

Human dynamics advisors. Human dynamics advisors have proven valuable, but the "cultural bench" is not as robust as needed to support the demand. Capability can be expanded both by improving professional military education and career paths, as well as by increasing collaboration and connectivity with experts outside DoD, both inside and outside of government. At the same time, future military leaders need to develop sufficient human dynamics astuteness in order to both request the support of human dynamics advisors and effectively consider the perspectives that they offer.

Science and technology investments. Coordination in the area of human dynamics S&T applies not only to ongoing programs but also to future investments. A better understanding is needed of current investments, current and future needs, and the gaps in between. "Gap analysis" can inform development of a science and technology investment strategy, overseen by a human dynamics "portfolio manager."

Data, tools, and products. While a large amount of human dynamics knowledge exists, it has been developed independently, tends to focus on specific users, and may not be maintained or well populated with current information. Attending to these shortfalls in a way that better integrates existing and future knowledge databases and tools so they are available to a broader base of users will facilitate development of expanded human dynamics capability.

High Priority Recommendations

The recommendations of this task force are grouped by six topics. All of these are important for the conflicts that the nation is likely to face in the next decade or two. However, four specific recommendations should have the highest priority in the near term as they provide the foundations for enabling all the rest. These four are:

- **Develop a comprehensive strategy**

- **Establish effective oversight**

- **Include specifically in oncoming QDR**

- **Increase the "cultural bench"**

Understanding human dynamics is a critical aspect of planning for success across the full spectrum of military and national security operations. While many perceive this as a new phenomenon, it has in fact been true for decades. During the Second World War and the reconstruction that followed, as well as during the Cold War, understanding human dynamics was considered essential. Collectively, the recommendations presented in this report will set the Department on a path toward enhancing the human dynamics capabilities within the military services, thereby better preparing our men and women in uniform for the operational environment of the future.

Appendix A. Definitions of Culture

Many definitions of culture exist, reflecting the views of different cultural theorists or particular areas of emphasis in the study of culture. Some common examples are illustrated in Figure A-1, and summarized in this appendix. In the figure, each line indicates the documents that describe culture, produced by a particular actor (Air Force, Marine Corps, Defense Intelligence Agency (DIA), and others). Those building blocks described by the most groups (five each) are: (1) beliefs, values, religion, and rituals; (2) norms and rules of behavior; and (3) the social network connecting individuals.

Figure A-1. Building Blocks of Cultures Described in DoD and Military Writings

While not explicitly stated in all definitions, the common view is that culture can be learned and is passed from one person to the next through interaction. All conceptions of culture consider multiple individuals, a transmission and learning process, a reinforcement process, and a notion of a partial sharing over the population. In the same population, two or more cultures can exist simultaneously, and individuals can be more or less associated with multiple cultures. Many definitions of culture discuss how it is created as groups go through common experiences and create shared memories, myths, and legends.

Most definitions describe how culture manifests itself in the roles that people take on, particularly as related to gender or family, power, the basis for trust, and the use of language. Cultural artifacts such as clothes, art, myths, legends, holidays, and symbols used in celebrations are often noted as outward signs of cultural differences. When two groups come into conflict, the two cultures may impact the nature and severity of the conflict. If one group continues to dominate, and its cultural artifacts begin to dominate, then, through a process called acculturation, the other group may come to adopt the dominant group's attitudes, beliefs, norms, and roles.

Definitions of Culture in the DoD

DoD field manuals offer several definitions of culture (Table A-1). At first glance it might seem that the DoD should adopt a common definition, taxonomy, and ontology for describing aspects of culture. Without a shared definition and ontology, the ability to link formal and computational models of culture to the wealth of cultural data collected in the field can be haphazard and some models will not be interoperable. Yet, this is a daunting task, as evidenced by the fact that the social sciences do not have a single uniformly agreed upon definition.

The diverse definitions of culture are driven by the fact that different groups have distinct needs for information. For example, the Marine Corps Intelligence Activity (MCIA) is driven by the need to provide the soldier with a snapshot of differences between other cultures and the United States. The anthropological human area file is driven by the need to collect comparable data.

It is unlikely that a single definition of culture will emerge, given that there is no common view as to why a single definition is needed. Rather than focusing on defining culture per se, the DoD may be better served by asking "what is it about culture that the soldier needs to know to improve performance at the tactical, operational, and/or strategic level?" At each level, different aspects of culture are mission critical.

For example, at the tactical level, understanding gender and family roles and how these are manifested in the way people dress, may save lives. At the strategic level, the key issue may be the dominant beliefs and attitudes that prevail and how well agreed upon they are in the population. From this perspective, the critical issue is not defining culture but identifying which manifestations need to be tracked to support mission objectives.

Table A-1. Culture Definitions Cited in DoD Manuals

US Army/Marine Corps Counterinsurgency Manual (FM 3-24)
3-37. Culture is "web of meaning" shared by members of a particular society or group within a society.
3-38. Culture might also be described as an "operational code" that is valid for an entire group of people.
Culture conditions the individual's range of action and ideas, including what to do and not do, how to do or not do it, and whom to do it with or not to do it with. Culture also includes under what circumstances the "rules" shift and change. Culture influences how people make judgments about what is right and wrong, assess what is important and unimportant, categorize things, and deal with things that do not fit into existing categories. Cultural rules are flexible in practice.

Psychological Operations Tactics, Techniques, and Procedures (FM 3-05.301/MCRP 3-40.6A)
Culture is—
- A system of shared beliefs, values, customs, behaviors, and artifacts that members of a society use to cope with their world and with one another.
- Learned, though a process called enculturation.
- Shared by members of a society; there is no "culture of one."
- Patterned, meaning that people in a society live and think in ways forming definite, repeating patterns.
- Changeable, through social interactions between people and groups.

Intelligence in Counterinsurgency
15 December 2006 FM 3-24/MCWP 3-33.5 3-7
- Arbitrary , meaning that Soldiers and Marines should make no assumptions regarding what a society considers right and wrong, good and bad.
- Internalized, in the sense that it is habitual, taken for granted, and perceived as "natural" by people within the society.

What follows is an illustrative set of definitions of culture, each of which is currently used in DoD by various entities and for different purposes. Many are embedded in the models, procedures, and tools being developed for or currently in use in the DoD.

Marine Corps Intelligence Activity

- Culture is the creation, maintenance, and transformation of semi-shared patterns of meaning, sense-making, affiliation, and organization by groups of people.

- It is a *continuing process* in which people interact with each other and with their environments.

- In addition, the MCIA provides an elaborate cultural taxonomy covering linguistic, gender, religious, health, and behavioral constraints, styles, and norms. This cultural taxonomy covers items not traditionally thought of as culture, such as organization of the military and demographics.

- By focusing on process, the MCIA definition opens the door to assessing how effects-based operations can change culture. However, the extensive taxonomy is so vague that it cannot be operationalized easily to support formal models. Data collected in this way will require substantial re-analysis by modelers.

Army Culture and Foreign Language Strategy

- Culture is the set of distinctive features of a society or group, including but not limited to values, beliefs, and norms, that ties together members of that society or group and that drives action and behavior.

- Culture is:
  - Learned and shared. There is no "culture of one."
  - Patterned, meaning that people in a group or society live and think in ways that form definitive, repeating patterns.
  - Challenged, through social interactions between people and groups.
  - Internalized, in the sense that it is habitual, taken for granted, and perceived as "natural" by people within the group or society.
  - Inclusive of particular myths and legends.

By focusing on specific features, this definition supports the development of models. Recognition that culture is learned supports the development of effects-based operations to change culture. The key difficulty is that the set of features is not well specified and some of those specified may be difficult to collect (e.g., myths and legends).

Defense Intelligence Definitions on Socio-Cultural Dynamics

The DIA-led Socio-Cultural Dynamics Working Group, whose membership comprises more than 30 organizations, has evolved as the mechanism in the defense intelligence community to handle the requirement for integrating foreign population and cultural-focused functional areas crossing multiple organizational boundaries and analytic competencies. The working group is the key component of the governance structure for developing a solution for managing socio-cultural dynamics across the defense intelligence enterprise. Along with DIA, the working group manages the federation of defense intelligence organizations performing socio-cultural dynamics analysis.

Defense intelligence has agreed on the following definitions for the defense intelligence enterprise:

- **Socio-cultural dynamics** is the information about the social, cultural, and behavioral factors characterizing the relationships and activities of the population of a specific region or operational environment.

- While terms including cultural geography, military geography, and human terrain are often considered synonymous, they are in fact subsets of the entire dynamic—a system that is constantly changing through time and across nation-state boundaries.

- The main intelligence analysis disciplines under socio-cultural dynamics are:

  - **Human factors**. The psychological, cultural, behavioral, and other human attributes that influence decision-making, information flow, and information interpretation by individuals or groups at any level in any state or organization.

- **Foreign culture analysis**. [All source analysis of] shared demographics, norms, values, institutions, and artifacts which assist in anticipating the actions of populations within the operating environment.
- **Human terrain analysis**. A multidisciplinary scientific approach to describe and predict geospatial and temporal patterns of human behavior by analyzing the attributes, actions, reactions, and interactions of groups or individuals in the context of their environment.

Special Forces

The Special Forces manual provides a very detailed discussion of culture from multiple theoretical perspectives. Key elements of culture are values, norms, institutions and artifacts. Culture is discussed as being partially shared, varying across the group, and learned.

Databases and Approaches

Numerous databases and approaches relate to cultural information. The two examples below are used by MCIA and DIA.

Standard Cross-Cultural Survey

The Standard Cross-Cultural Survey, developed by George Murdoch and others, includes information about 186 societies and 22 cultural categories, with almost one thousand standard coded variables derived from ethnographic sources (Murdoch and Morrow, 1970). The focus here is on characteristics of culture and the database enables cultural understanding through comparative analysis.

Hofstede

Hofstede characterizes culture along five dimensions: power distance, individualism, masculinity, uncertainty avoidance, and long-term orientation. Power distance is the extent to which less powerful members accept and expect that power is distributed unequally. It is a measure of acceptance of inequality and the presence of inequality. A culture is individualistic if each person is expected to look after him or herself and collectivistic if there is general socialistic oversight. Masculinity refers to the distribution of roles between the genders and the extent to which assertiveness, as opposed to feminine caring nurturing, norms dominate. Uncertainty avoidance is the extent to which a group can tolerate ambiguity and uncertainty. More structured ritualized groups have higher uncertainty avoidance. Long-term orientation is associated with thrift and perseverance; short-term orientation is associated with respect for tradition, fulfilling social obligations, and protecting one's "face."

"Culture is more often a source of conflict than of synergy. Cultural differences are a nuisance at best and often a disaster." (Prof. Geert Hofstede, Emeritus Professor, Maastricht University.)

Other Perspectives on Culture

Behavioral Perspective

The behavioral perspective conceives of culture as a set of codes of conduct, rituals, and tasks, as well as behavioral procedures, rules and norms. This is essentially identifying culture with its manifestations. Scholars who propose a behavioral perspective tend to identify organizational culture with its implications in terms of collective behavior. Joint actions, collective codes of conduct, rituals, and behavioral procedures are viewed as genuine forms of culture. The problem with this approach is that it does not explain what actually provides collective behavior with a cultural status. The hidden assumption here is that any diachronically consistent pattern of people's behavior counts as collective and, therefore, also cultural. However, consistency of behavior over time may well occur spontaneously, without the individuals being aware of, and having expectations about, each other's behavior. This is the case, for example, of a random collection of individuals who simultaneously need to come to grips with the same unexpected dangerous situation. In such circumstances, no one would arguably claim that consistency of behavior represents collective behavior, when in fact there is no actual social group whose members can view some form of behavior as "our" behavior.

Cognitive Perspective

The cognitive perspective identifies culture with people's perceptions, memories, shared understanding, beliefs, experiences, ideologies, and values. Scholars who endorse a cognitive perspective tend to identify culture with its content themes and patterns of interpretations or, more generally, with the object of people's mental attitudes. Typically, researchers with this perspective are interested in analyzing whether, and to what extent, culture, as a system of shared meanings and beliefs, can solve most of the ambiguities and conflict of interests that pervade organizational life. Moreover, they seek to explore the degree of differentiation and fragmentation between subcultures within organizations.

Such understanding has helped these scholars gain insight into the impact of culture upon organizational performance. For example, during the late 1970s and the early 1980s, scholars began to examine the impact of different national cultures on the operating characteristics of organizations, thereby bringing a new comparative international flavor to organizational research. However, despite the obvious theoretical importance of questions about culture and its effects on organizational performance, little rigorous or systematic analysis has been directed towards understanding the conditions under which a specific cognitive content becomes the object of culture to the point of being identified with culture itself.

Task Force Adopted Definition

In the context of this study, the task force defines **culture** as the collection of particular norms, beliefs, and customs held by every human, that impacts how individuals, groups, and societies behave and interact.

Appendix B. Insights from Past Experiences with Human Dynamics in Military Operations

All military operations have a critical human dimension. Though the nature, strength, and focus of human dynamics have varied across time and conflicts, their presence is undeniable. Human dynamics—as we have conceptualized them here—comprise the actions and interactions of personal, interpersonal, and social/contextual factors and their effects on behavioral outcomes.

Sun Tzu's ancient strategic admonition to "know your enemy" is axiomatic in military history, but historically many military leaders have interpreted this narrowly to mean that they should know (or have good intelligence preparation about) enemy fighting forces. In discussing contemporary military transformations, Steven P. Basilici and Jeremy Simmons have observed that the relevant scope of understanding should—perhaps must—also include cultural characteristics of the adversary:

> Understanding an adversary requires more than intelligence from three-letter agencies and satellite photos; it requires an understanding of their interests, habits, intentions, beliefs, social organizations, and political symbols—in other words, their culture. An American soldier can liken culture to a minefield: dangerous ground that, if not breached, must be navigated with caution, understanding, and respect. Cultural interpretation, competence, and adaptation are prerequisites for achieving a win-win relationship in any military operation. Operational commanders who do not consider the role of culture during mission planning and execution invite unintended and unforeseen consequences, and even mission failure.[53]

---

53 Basilici, Steven P. and Simmons, Jeremy (June, 2004). *Transformation: a bold case for unconventional warfare*. Naval Postgraduate School Monterey, California. p. 6.

For the military commander, however, understanding and mastering the human dimension of warfare—and Sun Tzu would probably agree—requires not only understanding these things about an "enemy," but also about the entire battlespace.

In his analysis of military leadership in the British Civil Wars, military historian Stanley D.M. Carpenter emphasizes the importance of an operation's "social context" and how this affects, and is affected by, force of human dynamics:

> Human dynamics encompass what Clausewitz called the 'moral forces' and include fear, motivation, passion, the urge to flee, hate, loyalty, and so on. A successful leader, through his inherent traits and behaviors, is able to overcome (or at least moderate) the negative aspects of human dynamics and conversely take advantage of the positive. In this regard, one can if not overcome, at least mitigate what Clausewitz popularized as the 'fog and friction of war'. It allows him to better manage the inherent chaos and uncertainty of combat. The societal context plays a large part in a military leader's success or failure. It often determines the quality of the instrument and certainly influences the depth of such human dynamics as motivation, passion, willingness to sacrifice and so forth. As with the human dynamics, it is how the commander, through his traits and behavior, manages the societal context that will determine his effectiveness.[54]

These pervasive human dynamics can be better understood to shape tactics and strategy. Indeed, the essence of strategy is to develop a plan of action that is likely to achieve a specific objective in light of an opponent's anticipated response. Anticipating responses—of an enemy, population, or social institution—has been a central dilemma of every military leader throughout history.

Some scholars of military strategy and history have suggested that, for the United States, strategy has been a core weakness. Colin Gray suggests that "The United States has a persisting strategy deficit. Americans are very competent at fighting, but they are much less

---

54. Carpenter, S. (2005). *Military Leadership in the British Civil Wars*, 1642-1651: The Genius of This Age. NY: Routledge. p. 5.

successful in fighting in such a way that they secure the strategic and, hence, political, rewards they seek."[55] It seems that the United States' past experiences with human dynamics in military operation illustrates the maxim that one can "win the battle (perhaps even all the battles) but lose the war."

Ideally, strategic competence evolves with experience. According to Gray, historical examination of past conflicts—of the U.S. and others—can help to redefine and improve the "American Way of Warfare." But he laments, "unfortunately, the first and truest love of the U.S. defense community is with technology, not with history." Gray's comments about the present parallel Ralph Peters' future-oriented analysis that "We need to struggle against our American tendency to focus on hardware and bean counting to attack the more difficult and subtle problems posed by human behavior and regional history."

History may lend its wisdom to understanding the role of human dynamics in military operations, but it certainly does not offer a menu of easy answers. Naval historian Geoffrey Till points out, however, that "The chief utility of history for the analysis of present and future lies in its ability, not to point out lessons, but to isolate things that need thinking about. … History provides insights and questions, not answers."[56] In that spirit, the following insights from past experience are offered for consideration.

Cultural Awareness Facilitates Strategic and Tactical Success

Examples of human dynamics affecting military operations are abundant—though largely anecdotal—and range from the micro to macro levels.

At the broadest, strategic level, Robert Jervis suggests that lack of cultural awareness is a major source of misperceptions between

---

55. Gray, Colin S. *Irregular Enemies and the Essence of Strategy: Can the American Way of War Adapt?* The Strategic Studies Institute, March 2006.
http://www.strategicstudiesinstitute.army.mil/pdffiles/pub650.pdf [January 2009]
56. Till, Geoffrey (1982). *Maritime Strategy and the Nuclear Age, London*: Macmillan, pp. 224–225.

nation/states (particularly as noted in the 1970s, between the United States and the Soviet Union), and that these misperceived intentions can have far-reaching consequences.[57] He rejects the more politically-oriented spiral and deterrence theories as explanations for Cold War escalations, and instead focuses on "psychological dynamics" as a source of cognitive bias that, unchecked, will create and sustain misperceptions. Those misperceptions form the basis for a state's decisions and subsequent actions.

Cooper and Telfer have analyzed the cultural impediments to effective relations and communication between the U.S. and Iran. They claim that these impediments create an environment that is not conducive to resolving its mutual, critical problems. They believe "the tragedy is that relations will deteriorate because the two nations, through a marked trend of political and strategic misperceptions, will be operating with false models of the political systems and organization of the other, leading to a state of confusion exacerbated by mutual incomprehension of each other's culture."[58]

At the ground level, among the most common examples for the U.S. military are foibles and missteps arising from a lack of cultural awareness. Skelton and Cooper provide a concise description of the problem and the call for a solution:

> Few members of the Armed Forces will be familiar with cultural traditions of the countries in which they operate. Yet violation of local norms and beliefs can turn a welcoming population into a hostile mob. Iraqis arrested by U.S. troops have had their heads forced to the ground, a position forbidden by Islam except during prayers. This action offends detainees as well as bystanders. In Bosnia, American soldiers angered Serbs by greeting them with the two-fingered peace sign, a gesture commonly used by their Croat enemies. And the circled-finger "A–OK" signal was a gross

---

57. Jervis, Robert. "Hypotheses on Misperception," *World Politics*, Vol. 20, No. 3 (April 1968), p. 454-479. Jervis, Robert. *Perception and Misperception in International Politics.* New Jersey: Princeton University Press (1976).
58. Cooper, A. and Telfer, L. (Summer 2006). "Misperceptions and Impediments in the US-Iran Relationship." *49th Parallel: An Interdisciplinary Journal of North American Studies, Conference Special Edition.* p. 27.

insult to Somalis. The military has enough to worry about without alienating the local population. … It is clear that the Armed Forces lack sophisticated knowledge of foreign countries. That does not dishonor their performance; cultural awareness is not a mission-essential task—but it should be.[59]

These cultural violations seem to have the most significant impact in operations that require engagement with a host population and that support stability or humanitarian assistance activity. One insight from these experiences seems to be the need to define the "battlespace," terrain, or area of operation, not just by physical or geographic boundaries, but also by culture. This means that service members must not only train to "know the enemy," but to "know the area." Most of Arcuri's examples are not mistakes in anticipating an enemy maneuver, they are social/cultural mistakes that carried the potential not only to anger and embolden the adversary, but also to cultivate broad hostility among the population toward U.S. presence and personnel. That hostility could then complicate current mission objectives and future operational planning.

The examples do illustrate, however, that the effects of cultural awareness (or lack thereof) can be expected to influence mission effectiveness even at the most minute and incidental tactical level. This does not mean that each soldier, sailor, airman, and marine must be an expert in the area of operation, but basic cultural awareness should be a fundamental skill for all troops operating in a foreign environment.

It is Necessary to Understand and Accept that Military Operations Have Political Objectives and Effects

War and politics are inextricably linked. This principle is found in most theories of warfare and evidence of its truth has been found in virtually every known military conflict. Clausewitz—the deeply influential Prussian military theorist—said starkly that "war is a

---

59. Skelton, Ike and Jim Cooper. "You're Not from Around Here, Are You?" *Joint Forces Quarterly* (36), December 2004. http://www.ndu.edu/inss/press/jfq_pages/0436.pdf

continuation of politics with other means." Chairman Mao Tse-Tung commented similarly on the relationship, claiming: "Politics is war without bloodshed while war is politics with bloodshed."

While the confluence of politics and war may seem an obvious point, it is not one that many American policy-makers seem ready to accept. Jeffrey Record observes that "Permeating the entire fabric of America's strategic culture and approach to war, especially the aversion to fighting for limited political purposes, is an unwillingness to accept war as a continuation of politics."[60] Record further opines that "This insistence on politically immaculate military operations underpins the conventional wisdom in the United States regarding the failed prosecution of the Vietnam War." When nations oppose nations with conventional force, the power of political will and popular support favor the U.S., but when the America becomes involved in "small wars," foreign insurgencies, and humanitarian intervention (what many see as the future of warfare), the "political" objectives become less palatable, though operationally essential.

Historically, when a third-party nation has stepped in to help suppress an insurgency, the "successful" cases nearly always involve important political concessions (to the insurgents' interest) by the indigenous government. Concessions were designed specifically to address insurgent grievances and offered even when the counterinsurgency was not favoring the indigenous government. In the Mau Mau Uprising (1952-1960), for example, concessions were made for land reform and voting rights. During The Malayan Emergency (1948-60) the government critically conceded freedom from British rule, voting rights, and actions to relieve the effects of long-term bigotry on the ethnic Chinese population.

Making concessions can be difficult to "sell" politically to the people of an intervening government. These concessions, however, were not intended as a form of surrender or a sign of weakness, but rather as an essential way to dry up popular support for the insurgents. They were apparently effective for that purpose. Because political

---

60. Record, Jeffrey. September 1, 2006. "The American Way of War: Cultural Barriers to Successful Counterinsurgency," Cato Institute Paper, no. 577; 1-20. p. 5.

factors are so important for the success of military operations, the *population,* not just the enemy, becomes a vital concern.

Populations Matter As Much As (Sometimes More Than) Fighting Forces in Determining Military Success

Historically, during conventional wars there has been a dominant—in some cases, nearly exclusive—focus on understanding and countering enemy military forces. What has been lost is the critical importance of understanding and influencing the population. As the U.S. has become increasingly involved in "small wars" and various forms of irregular warfare around the globe, the essential role of a population in military operations—though known for centuries—has again come more sharply into view.

In the early 1800s, Napoleon Bonaparte, an imposing conventional warrior and military strategist, failed to understand—or even seek to understand—the culture of the battlespace as he preemptively invaded Spain and Portugal. With ease, his occupying military forces strode into the region and dethroned the royal family. His victory seemed effortless and complete.

Napoleon anticipated and conquered the formal state governing structure, but he failed to learn in advance how little control that authority held over large segments of its populace. Residents of the Navarre region, in particular, had become heavily dependent economically on illicit foreign trade and had a great deal to lose from the prospect of new, foreign governance. They also were more deeply bound to the influences of the Catholic Church, than Napoleon realized. According to Chandler, the confluence of forces cultivated within the population—foreseeable, but unforeseen—included "popular patriotism, religious fanaticism, and an almost hysterical hatred for the French."[61] That dynamic transformed Napoleon's

---

61. Chandler, David G. (1966). *The Campaigns of Napoleon.* New York: Simon and Schuster, p. 659.

graceful occupation into a protracted eight-year, resource-consuming struggle.

According to Smith: "The strategic gap that developed between Napoleon's rapid conventional military victory and the immediate requirement to influence positively the population as part of post-hostilities stabilization operations highlights the limits of conventional military power in post-conflict operations and the perils of forgetting "the people" in the initial and ongoing strategic calculus. Unfortunately, nations and militaries around the globe have been forced to relearn that lesson many times in the ensuing 200 years."[62]

Accounting, as Smith says, for "the people" in initial and ongoing strategic planning requires understanding and anticipating their role both in resistance and in resolution. One of the longstanding maxims of counterinsurgency strategy is to separate the population from the insurgents. This is done to increase physical and informational control; to stem the tide of insurgent growth and recruitment by denying them access; to permit kinetic action against insurgents that occurs "out of view" of the populace and reduces risk of collateral injuries; and to increase the population's sense of security, at least within their "safe zones." Andrew F. Krepinevich suggests that neglecting this separation principle was a major downfall in the United States' military action in Vietnam. He concludes that superior U.S. firepower facilitated massive Viet Cong attrition, but "it never denied the enemy his source of strength—access to the people."[63]

When insurgents have easy access to, and are hopelessly co-mingled with, the population, it is easier for them to control the "narrative" of what is happening. When the insurgent view becomes ground truth for the population, the resistance not only gains new fighters, but just as importantly, it gains a broader base of sympathizers. A population of sympathizers is perhaps the most powerful force multiplier for insurgents.

---

62. Smith, George (2004). *Avoiding a Napoleonic Ulcer: Bridging the Gap of Cultural Intelligence.* CJCS Strategy Essay Competition. Washington D.C: National Defense University Press. p. 22.
63. Krepinevich, Andrew (1986). *The Army and Vietnam.* Baltimore, MD: The Johns Hopkins Press. p. 197.

During World War II, as part of the People's Liberation War of Yugoslavia, the Yugoslavian Partisans enjoyed tremendous growth and success (culminating in over three quarters of a million fighting troops)—according to a former embedded OSS officer, Franklin Lindsay—largely as a function of a friendly population. Lindsay says of the populace that "Their support was crucial to success. They provided the intelligence screens that surrounded and protected the armed Partisans, as well as the food and clothing, the shelter and the recruits, without which the Partisans could not survive."[64] T. E. Lawrence similarly noted that "Rebellions can be made by two percent active in a striking force, and 98 percent passively sympathetic."[65]

Continuity of Knowledge on Human Dynamics is Essential, Particularly in Joint/Coalition and Protracted Operations.

During the U.S. "RESTORE HOPE" operations in Somalia (UN Operation in Somalia, UNOSUM I), the first Joint Force Commander recognized the grave operational implications of the region's "clan warfare" culture and tasked the 1st Marine Expeditionary Force to monitor not only adversary intent, but also the "disposition" of the population. A Joint Universal "lessons learned" analysis says of the Somalis that "their culture stresses the idea of 'me and my clan against all outsiders,' with alliances between clans being only temporary conveniences. Guns and aggressiveness, including the willingness to accept casualties, are intrinsic parts of this culture, with women and children considered part of the clan's order of battle."[66]

These issues proved to be vital for operational planning. Unfortunately, the cultural lessons devolved over time and across changes in personnel to the extent that "during UNOSOM II, U.S. leaders failed to take certain factors of Somali culture into

---

64. Lindsay, Franklin (1993). *Beacons in the Night: With the OSS and Tito's Partisan's in Wartime Yugoslavia.* Stanford: Stanford University Press. p. 198.
65. Quoted in Laqueur, W. (Ed.) (2004). *Voices of terror: Manifestos, writings and manuals of Al Qaeda, Hamas, and other terrorists from around the world and throughout the ages.* New York: Reed Press.
66. Allard, Kenneth (1995). *Somalia Operations: Lessons Learned.* Washington DC: National Defense University Press. p. 13.

consideration, contributing to the operation's failure."[67] As Kent Strader observes: "Somewhere in the transfer of authority (TOA) between UNOSUM I and II knowledge was lost or ignored."[68]

The "lessons learned" analysis concludes that "The Somalia experience underlines the importance of knowing the country, the culture, the ground, and the language as a pre-condition for military operations," but an embedded insight is that continuity of knowledge is important.[69] Senior command certainly must understand the cultural and other human dynamics of the battlespace, but the responsibility for this knowledge cannot be relegated solely to the operational commander.[70] As experiences in Iraq show, even brigade-level leaders must ensure that human dynamics intelligence has continuity through the transfer of authority. Brigades and their units frequently experience deployment rotations or geographic displacements. What is learned about the battlespace in one area or on one deployment may not apply when the same unit moves just thirty miles away. It is critical that area-specific knowledge not only be collected and used, but also shared and preserved through changes in personnel.

Human Dynamics Are Fluid and Often Variable Across and Within Conflicts or Operations

Past experiences suggest that human dynamics largely shape the disposition of a population and the character of conflict. In his book, *Battle: A History of Combat and Culture*, John Lynn argues that all warfare is, and has been, culture-specific. He suggests that since Ancient Greek times, dynamics of human values, expectations and preconceptions—cultural (a term he uses to refer to a complex that is somewhat more idiosyncratic than nomothetic) dynamics in particular—have been the

---

67. U.S. Department of Defense, JP 3-06, Doctrine for Joint Urban Operations (Washington, D.C.: Government Printing Office, 16 September 2002), III-10.
68. Strader, O. Kent (2006). *Culture: The New Key Terrain—Integrating Cultural Competence into JIPB.* School of Advanced Military Studies, United States Army Command and General Staff College, Fort Leavenworth, Kansas. p. 27.
69. *Ibid.*, p. 95.
70. Gordon, James A. (2004). *Cultural Assessments and Campaign Planning: A Monograph.* School of Advanced Military Studies, United States Army Command and General Staff College, Fort Leavenworth, Kansas.

principal driver of whether and how nations have engaged in armed conflict.[71] While Lynn's argument is somewhat polemic, he provides extensive examples to support his view from conflicts and eras throughout military history. He concludes that human dynamics influences have been not only robust in warfare, but that the dynamics and their effects varied with the culture of the conflict's participants.

In his landmark analysis of the Vietnam War, Douglas Pike reaches a similar conclusion: that unconventional warfare does not lend itself to a grand theory. Each conflict or operation possesses a unique set of causes and sustaining or driving factors. One size—or one understanding—does not fit all. Pike concludes that "Unconventional wars grow because of the peculiar political soil of individual cultures."[72] If this is true, then according to Kent Strader, a key to success for the operational commander will be "to unravel the cause of conflict and attack its origins with non-kinetic tools and to a lesser degree its soldiers."[73]

Past military experience does not indicate that *no* human dynamics are persistent or enduring, only that many are unique and/or variable both across and even within a given operation. It is reasonable to infer that certain core dynamics are recurrent across most conflicts. However, even the core dynamics, which are relatively stable, are transformative. That is, the core dynamic may persist, but its manifestations may be different depending on contextual influences, and they change over the developmental course of the operation.

One of the predominant core dynamics influencing a population is its perceived safety and security. Perhaps this principle is not surprising. It has been a cornerstone of behavioral theories of motivation for more than half a century. Nearly every college student has been exposed to Abraham Maslow's "hierarchy of needs," in which safety/security is just one motivational notch above a human's physiological needs for

---

71. Lynn, John (2003). *Battle: A History of Combat and Culture from Ancient Greece to Modern America.* New York: Westview Press.
72. Pike, Douglas (1986). *PAVN: People's Army of Vietnam,* Novato, CA: Presidio Press. p. 54.
73. Strader, O. Kent (2006). p. 25

food, sleep, etc.[74] In nearly all known military operations, securing the population's sense of safety has been a necessary (though not always sufficient) condition for any successful campaign to win its "hearts and minds." People feel safer living in an environment that they perceive as orderly, predictable, and fair. When an occupying military can provide that environment for the population, the loyalty of the people often follows. Without it, however, it has faltered.

Though a population's sense of security is a robust contributor to operational success, its manifestations are transformative, and therefore, fluid. In past military conflicts, the nature and object of safety concerns has evolved over time. A population may begin by fearing threats from a repressive government, but over time becomes more concerned about protection against accidental and intentional harm from insurgents who are resisting an occupying force. Likewise, in human terrain relief operations and stability operations, safety needs may shift from an initial focus on protection against tribal or sectarian violence to protection against disease and health concerns—or vice versa. The same "dynamic" or need is manifested in a different form and may require a different military response. That even the "stable" dynamics are fluid means—consistent with the "continuity" insight—that monitoring the disposition of the population must be ongoing and continuous.

Finally, it is striking how the influence of human dynamics in military operations can vary widely even *within* a given conflict or *within* the battlespace. This insight has been dramatically evident throughout recent U.S. experiences in Iraq. David Kilcullen—the senior counterinsurgency strategy advisor in the United States—based on personal experiences and observation notes that "Knowledge of Iraq is very time-specific and location-specific. ... Hence, observations from one time/place may or may not be applicable elsewhere, even in the same campaign in the same year: we must first understand the essentials of the environment, then determine whether analogous situations exist, before attempting to apply "lessons.""[75]

---

74. Maslow, A.H. (1943). A Theory of Human Motivation, *Psychological Review* 50, 370-96.

75. Kilcullen, David (2007). *Counterinsurgency in Iraq: Theory and Practice*, 2007.

This has serious implications for the depth and frequency of intelligence assessments, within-theatre information sharing, and the aforementioned continuity and transfer of knowledge.

Appendix C. Formal Requirements and Perceived Needs

Human Dynamics in DoD Directives, Doctrine, and Policy Documents

Every briefing received by the task force supported the need and criticality for increased knowledge of human dynamics in current and future military operations. However, a review of formally stated requirements of combatant commands and current Department of Defense directives and instructions do not clearly establish the need or the direction for programs dealing with human dynamics. At best, the need to understand human dynamics for various military operations are implied rather than stated.

A comprehensive review of Joint Publication 1-02, the *DoD Dictionary of Military and Associated Terms*, dated 12 April 2001, as amended through 04 March 2008, revealed no listing of human dynamics, human terrain, or cultural awareness. Interestingly, "culture" is defined in this publication in only the geographical sense as: "A feature of the terrain that has been constructed by man. Included are such items as roads, buildings, and canals; boundary lines; and, in a broad sense, all names and legends on a map."

A clearly defined and understood definition of human dynamics and the relevant aspects of culture is essential to coordinating different research, collection, analysis, and development of human dynamics material.

There are five DoD directives and one instruction that address or imply the need for understanding human dynamics. These are:

- DoD Directive 2000.13, Subject: Civil Affairs, dated 27, 1994.

- DoD Directive 3000.05, Subject: Military Support for Stability, Security, Transition, and Reconstruction (SSTR) Operations, November 28, 2005.

- DoD Directive O-3600.01, Subject: Information Operations (IO), August 14, 2006.

- DoD Directive 3305.6, Subject: Special Operations Forces Foreign Language Policy, January 4, 1993.

- DoD Instruction 1315.20, Subject: Management of Department of Defense (DoD) Foreign Area Officer (FAO) Programs, September 28, 2007.

The following excerpts from these DoD documents address or imply the need for understanding human dynamics.

- The **Civil Affairs Directive** (2000.13) establishes policy to "Minimize, to the extent feasible, civilian interference with military operations and the impact of military operations on the civilian population" and to "Provide assistance to meet the life-sustaining needs of the civilian population." Both of these require knowledge of the culture and human dynamics to succeed. As an example, U.S. forces would be better prepared to provide life sustaining assistance if they understood the dietary restrictions of the population and the dynamics of the food distribution system.

- The **Military Support for SSTR Operations Directive** (3000.05) contains numerous references to the need for understanding human dynamics. Furthermore, responsibilities and taskings are identified that are applicable to understanding human dynamics. The following examples from 3000.5, with the paragraph numbers indicated, show the relationship to human dynamics:

  - 4.1. Stability operations are a core U.S. military mission … They shall be … integrated across all DoD activities …

  - 4.2. The long-term goal is to help develop indigenous capacity for security essential services, a viable market economy, rule of law, democratic institutions, and a robust civil society.

  - 4.3.1 Rebuild indigenous institutions …

- ▪ 4.3.2 Revive or build the private sector, including encouraging citizen-driven, bottom-up economic activity and constructing necessary infrastructure … .

- ▪ 4.11 Stability operations skills, such as foreign language capabilities, regional area expertise, and experience with foreign governments and International Organizations, shall be developed and incorporated into Professional Military Education at all levels.

- ▪ 5.1.8. Create a stability operations center to coordinate stability operations research, education and training, and lessons-learned.

- ▪ 5.2.2. [The Under Secretary of Defense for Intelligence shall] ensure the availability of suitable intelligence … resources for stability operations, including the ability to rapidly stimulate intelligence gathering and assign … skilled … personnel to such missions.

- The **Special Operations Forces (SOF) Foreign Language Policy Directive** (3305.6) establishes policy to have SOF organizations develop foreign language skills.

- The **Information Operations Directive** (O-3600.01) states (in paragraph 4.2.4) "Intelligence shall be developed … to provide data about adversary information systems or networks; produce political-military assessments; conduct human factors analysis; and provide indications and warning of adversary IO, including threat assessments."

- The **Management of DoD Foreign Area Officer Programs Instruction** (1315.20) establishes policy that FAOs will possess a unique combination of strategic focus, regional expertise (including cultural awareness) and foreign language proficiency.

There are other DoD directives and instructions that imply the need for information on human dynamics or culture in a foreign country. For example, DoD Directive 2205.2, Subject: Humanitarian and Civic Assistance Provided in Conjunction with Military Operations, October 6, 1994; and DoD Directive 5100.46, Subject: Foreign Disaster Relief, December 4, 1975, would require information about the human dynamics or culture in a foreign country to plan operations that are effective.

Doctrine also exists to reinforce the need for information on human dynamics. The best illustration of existing doctrine is found in Joint Publication 3-57, *Joint Doctrine for Civil-Military Operations*. This publication contains insightful guidance on collecting human dynamic and cultural data for use in civil-military operations and calls for the collection of information on these considerations:

- political
- economic
- military
- health services
- paramilitary
- environmental
- ethnic
- criminal
- religious

The task force also noted the stated need for increased cultural awareness and language training in the 2006 Quadrennial Defense Review. Under the section concerning *Developing a 21st Century Total Force*, the QDR states, "Developing broader linguistic capability and cultural understanding is also critical to prevail in the long war and to meet 21st century challenges." (p. 78) There are six desires following that statement. All six deal with language skills, but none of them specifically discuss ways of achieving other cultural awareness knowledge or to reach those that are unable to attain language proficiency related to a specific population they have to work with.

The QDR is neither a formal requirements nor a resource document. Accordingly, and at best, it implies (rather than tasks) that DoD organizations should undertake programs to achieve better cultural awareness other than through language training.

Requirements Derived from Experience

Virtually every briefing received by the task force contained quotes, innuendoes, and anecdotal information referring to the need for programs to collect, analyze, produce product, educate, train, and better plan military operations using human dynamics information. It became very evident to the task force that different audiences (users) have different needs based on their interactions with persons of other cultures. The audiences can be categorized as follows:

- Positional authority

  - In general, positional authority and responsibilities will characterize the type and depth of information related to cultural considerations. For example, high ranking officials (*e.g.*, flag officers) are infrequently involved with close contact with an indigenous populace. On the other hand, a non-commissioned officer assigned advisory responsibilities may have to live and work with indigenous personnel on a 24/7 basis.

  - A higher ranking person may enjoy the luxury of having time to prepare for a meeting with indigenous personnel. They can be briefed on specific items of human dynamics and culture that will help them succeed and to leave a good impression with the indigenous personnel.

  - In contrast, the person living and working with indigenous persons on a 24/7 basis has a greater need for detailed information that assists that person in accomplishing his/her mission. The person in this situation is under continual scrutiny by those he/she is working with or leading, and any violations of culturally sensitive taboos are exacerbated.

  - Regardless, both high ranking officials and those of lesser rank can profit from increased awareness of understanding the human dynamics in a particular population. The principal differences are in the amount of preparation and the depth and type of knowledge that must be possessed.

- Organizational mission focus

  - Organizations such as the Army's Special Operations Command, along with its Special Forces Command and Civil Affairs and Psychological Operations Command, have an inherent need to understand human dynamics to meet their mission requirements. Accordingly, they appear to view collection, analysis, and dissemination of such information as a critical need for mission success, although it is an informal requirement.

- Other Service field organizations whose missions bring them in close and continuing contact with those from other cultures have learned or relearned their need to understand human dynamics because Operations Enduring Freedom and Iraqi Freedom have required them to work more closely with foreign cultures.

- The task force encountered numerous references to the differences in informational needs depending on the phase (or type) of operation they were conducting. For example, the initial military objectives and mission concentration at the start of Operation Iraqi Freedom called for the destruction of Iraqi military forces. Admirably, U.S. and coalition forces destroyed standard Iraqi forces rapidly and effectively. The need for understanding human dynamics and cultural information was reduced during this phase. As our standard forces transitioned to a security, stability, and reconstruction role, their need for cultural awareness information increased exponentially.

- Frequency and type of contact with other cultures

  - Higher ranking officials may be able to live with generalized information about an overall culture, *e.g.*, general information on tribes in Iraq. However, the person tasked with working with a particular tribal grouping must not only understand the dynamics of that tribe, but those of other tribal groupings that drive interactions and success of different endeavors.

Appendix D. Current DoD Efforts

The broad spectrum of divergent missions facing today's military, ranging from multinational and domestic terrorism to stability operations, humanitarian efforts, and disaster relief, dictates that DoD must re-evaluate its short and long-term commitments and investments related to human dynamics and social-behavioral needs, in support of its operations.

The task force attempted to gain an understanding of the current efforts and investments and did so from four directions:

- data call by the Office of the Secretary of Defense

- knowledge of the individual members and government advisors

- briefings to the task force (see list later in this report)

- investigations by individual members of the task force

The picture that emerged was a widely scattered set of efforts and investments with no single (or few) point(s) of coordination or oversight, and no coherent plan for dealing with this critically important area. As a result, those efforts identified and outlined in this appendix must be viewed as illustrative examples, but not considered as a comprehensive list. There is a lot going on. There are many efforts trying to address elements of the problem and apparently some good work in progress or in the field (the "thousand flowers" situation).

The chaotic approach that we observed was appropriate as a response to "the moment of need," although it would clearly have been better to have preserved the requisite capabilities from prior conflicts. However, it is now time to introduce some semblance of coherence and top-down guidance as recommended earlier in this report.

The balance of this appendix summarizes the efforts identified by the task force and, as indicated above, should be viewed as illustrative of on-going efforts.

Data Call and Response

The data call sent out at the request of the task force is shown in Figure D-1. The unclassified responses are summarized in Table D-1.

DoD Programs

Table D-2, provided by OASD (NII), contains examples of programs in the Office of the Secretary of Defense, defense agencies, and joint environment. It includes efforts for social-behavioral modeling and simulation, field applications, and training. There is some overlap between Tables D-1 and D-2.

Service Programs

The military services have reacted to the needs in Afghanistan and Iraq, though belatedly. To a large degree, the resulting efforts are similar to those built and forgotten from previous conflicts (such as Vietnam). A number of programs reviewed by the task force are discussed in Chapter 5, Education, Training, and Expertise.

DEFENSE SCIENCE
BOARD

MEMORANDUM FOR SECRETARIES OF THE MILITARY DEPARTMENTS
CHAIRMAN OF THE JOINT CHIEFS OF STAFF
UNDER SECRETARY OF DEFENSE FOR POLICY
UNDER SECRETARY OF DEFENSE FOR PERSONNEL
AND READINESS
COMMANDERS OF THE COMBATANT COMMANDS
DIRECTOR OF THE DEFENSE INTELLIGENCE AGENCY
DIRECTOR NATIONAL GEOSPATIAL INTELLIGENCE
AGENCY
DIRECTOR OF THE NATIONAL SECURITY AGENCY
DIRECTOR OF THE DEFENSE ADVANCED RESEARCH
PROJECTS AGENCY
DIRECTOR OF THE DEFENSE THREAT REDUCTION
AGENCY
DIRECTOR OF THE JOINT IMPROVISED EXPLOSIVE
DEVICE DEFEAT ORGANIZATION

SUBJECT: Defense Science Board Task Force on Understanding Human Dynamics

The Defense Science Board (DSB) serves as an advisory body to the Secretary of
Defense on matters relating to scientific, technical and policy matters. A DSB Task
Force, under the sponsorship of the USD(P) and the USD(AT&L), was established to
study Understanding Human Dynamics/Human Terrain. The evolving scope of U.S.
activities world-wide has highlighted the importance of understanding the cultures of
friends and adversaries, especially for deployed forces. As part of the data gathering
portion in this endeavor, the Task Force requests you identify projects and programs for
FY07-09 (if any) aimed at increasing the understanding of various cultures and
environments and its applications, including operations and training.

This Task Force will focus on technical/operational applications (as opposed to
strategic communication or non-state WMD issues) relating to understanding human
dynamics. We request that you provide a short paragraph on each effort or group of
efforts that either builds a science or technology foundation or is mostly directed at

Figure D-1. Data Call Request

tactical/operational applications of human dynamics/human terrain/culture including the following categories:

- Science and technology of human dynamics/terrain/culture
  - includes social and behavioral sciences
  - excludes human computer interaction and human effectiveness
- Intelligence
  - data collection
  - analysis and studies
- Modeling and simulation
- Operational programs (such as the Human Terrain System)
- Training
  - foreign language
  - culture
  - adversary

Please concentrate efforts to those programs focused on helping operational units in the field. For each effort or group of efforts under the same sponsorship, indicate the approximate level of effort for FY07, FY08, and FY09, measured in man-years or dollars (or both), as appropriate. We have provided a sample table below for reference.

We request that you provide this data by February 29, 2008. Your inputs will be consolidated and used in a final report that will go to the Secretary of Defense and other senor DoD leadership.

My point of contact for this effort is Mr. Dave Sobyra, OASD SO/LIC, (703) 697-5447, e-mail david.sobyra@osd.mil and SIPRNET at david.sobyra@osd.smil.mil.

	Brief Description	Category	Fiscal Year 2008		Fiscal Year 2009	
			Man-years	Contract $	Man-years	Contract $

William Schneider, Jr.
Chairman

2

Figure D-1. Data Call Request (continued)

Table D-1. Summary of Data Call Responses

Organization	Effort	Category
JIEDDO	Human Terrain System	Operational
	Red Team	Threat emulation
	Social Network Analysis	Analysis and S&T
	Social forces workshop	Threat analysis & modeling
	XVIII ABC Corps Assessment Cell	Threat analysis & modeling
	Understanding operational environment	S&T
	Understanding threat behaviors	S&T and threat modeling
U.S. Special Operations Command (SOCOM)	Human terrain & social network analysis	Operational
	SKOPE	Analysis
	Center for excellence for IR & UW	Culture analysis
	Influence operations	IO & psychological operations (PSYOPS)
	Joint Warfare Analysis Center/SIGINT Control and Analysis Module	M&S
	Geospatial & data mining for intelligence	Operational
U.S. Strategic Command (STRATCOM) /SOCOM	Human Network Attack Initiative - social network analysis - planning tools - human terrain mapping	Operational
U.S. Strategic Command	Strategic deterrence assessment lab (behavioral sciences)	Analysis
	Psychological operations Joint Munitions Effectiveness Manual functional area	Analysis
U.S. Southern Command	Core capabilities for tactical social science and regional experts (with DIA)	Intelligence
	Understanding geospatial and temporal patterns of human behavior (with NGA)	Intelligence
	Network studies, research, intelligence analysis, strategic culture	Operational
U.S. Central Command	Mapping human terrain joint capability technology demonstration	Operational research and development
	Human Terrain Teams	Operational
	Human dynamics/terrain/culture S&T	S&T
	Human Terrain System toolkits	Operational
	Socio-cultural dynamics working group	DIA led

Table D-1. Summary of Data Call Responses (continued)

Organization	Effort	Category
National Geospatial-Intelligence Agency	Human Terrain Analysis Pilot	S&T and intelligence
	Topnymic Program (geographic names)	Intelligence
	Political Boundary Collection & Analysis	Intelligence
	Geographic names & international boundary trainers	Training
	Analyst training in foreign languages and regional cultures	Training
	Geographic-information-system-based analysis via spatial modus operandi	S&T
	Human language processing technology	Operational
Army	HTS (TRADOC led)	Operational
	Mapping human terrain toolkit	Operational
	TRADOC Intelligence Support Activity Modeling & Simulation	Operational
	Human dynamic & cross-cultural competence at Army Research Institute	S&T
	Geo-cultural analysis tool	S&T
	Irregular Warfare Network Analysis	Analysis and studies
	Middle East Cultural Integration Course	Training
	Culture and foreign language strategy	Training
	University of foreign military & cultural studies	Training
	Sequoyah Foreign Language Translation System	Operational
	Every Soldier is a Sensor training support pkg	Training
	Military intelligence foreign language training center	Training
	Visualization of Belief Systems	Research and development
	Army Cultural Summit (March 08)	Review on-going efforts
North Command/ American Aerospace Defense U.S. Northern Command	Human interoperability	Planning and analysis
	HTT in Mexico for stability operations	Planning
	U.S. Northern Command area of responsibility culture training course	Training

Table D-1. Summary of Data Call Responses (continued)

Organization	Effort	Category
U.S. Joint Forces Command (JFCOM)	Global Synchronization Tool in Support of Global War on Terror	Operational
	Theater Effects Based Operations	Operational
	Modeling and simulation	M&S
	Field Experiment: Commander, International Security Assistance Force X	Operational, M&S
	Integrated Battle Command Tool	Operational, M&S
SOAL-T	Clandestine Tagging, Tracking & Locating	Intelligence
	Nano-technology Integration	Intelligence
	Nano enabled TTL (transistor-transistor logic) devices	Intelligence
	3-D Facial Recognition Imaging Technology	Intelligence
	Counterintelligence – Human Intelligence Advanced Modernization Program	Operational
	Psyop Global Reach	Operational
	Identify and track important asses	Intelligence
	Automated detection and cueing	Intelligence
	Tactical biometric registration/recognition	Intelligence
	Interactive language trainer	Training
	3-D facial imaging system	Intelligence
	Cultural intelligence wiki-berry	Intelligence
SOJICC	Advanced Remote Ground Unattended Sensor Systems – Knowledge discovery - RDEC (social network analysis) - Emergent leader analysis - Pattern Detection Facility - Interagency task force geospatial initiative	Operational
	Combined Theater Analyst Vetted, Relational Structure	Intelligence
	Open source intelligence section	Intelligence
	Joint intelligence preparation of the operational environment	Intelligence
	Strategic multilayered assessment for weapons of mass destruction (WMD) terrorism	Intelligence
U.S. Marine Corps	Basic school and CAOCL	Training
	Center for adv operational culture learning	Training
	Expeditionary Warfare School	Training
	MCIA culture intelligence products	Intelligence
	Language training	Training
Office of Naval Intelligence	Introduction to cultural analytics	Training

Table D-1. Summary of Data Call Responses (continued)

Organization	Effort	Category
Office of the Chief of Naval Operations, N27 (Naval Intelligence)	Naval intelligence basic course-geopolitical analysis	Training
Naval Surface Warfare Center	Pre-deployment training - Afghanistan, Iraq, middle east region	
Navy Language Skills, Regional Expertise and Cultural Awareness	Operational cultural & language familiarization	Training
	Navy intelligence foreign language program	Training
Navy Expeditionary Combat Command	Cultural sensitivity training	Training
	Regional orientation with survival language	Training
	Immersion language class	Training
	Cultural sensitivity training	Training
Commander, Navy Installations Command	4 courses	Training
Naval Post Graduate School	Regional security education program	Training
Office of Naval Research	Social networks	S&T
	Modeling asymmetric adversaries	S&T
	Insurgent groups as emergent systems	S&T
	Moral values and terrorist activity	S&T
	Human activity recognition	S&T
	Smart Fence (acoustic detection)	S&T
	Modeling of adaptive asymmetric tactics	S&T
	Base Protection ("anomalous" behavior	S&T
	NonKin Village training game	Training
	Naval education and training command (NETC): Detainee overview	Training
	NETC: cultural awareness	Training
	NETC: Middle east and Islamic cultures	Training
	NETC: Individual augmentation course	Training
	Naval War College	Training

Table D-1. Summary of Data Call Responses (continued)

Organization	Effort	Category
Air Force	Target analysis of individual terrorist signature	S&T
	Behavior signature readers: diagnostic tools for inferring personal variables from behavior	S&T
	Sense making support environment	S&T
	Unified behavior signatures creation and use	S&T
	Simulation of cultural identities for prediction of reactions	S&T
	Human & system and modeling analysis toolkit	S&T
	PSYOPS target analysis of individuals: Social network analyses of adversaries	S&T
	Cyber target characterization	S&T
	Automated speech recognition and audio retrieval	S&T
	Air advisor training	Training
	Language and cultural training	Training

Table D-2. Current DoD Efforts, OSD Perspective

OSD/Agency/Service Efforts

- Social-Cultural Dynamics Initiative (DIA)
- Social Science Research and Analysis Council (OUSD (Policy))
- Human Interoperability Enterprise (OASD (NII))
- Social-Behavioral Efforts (OSD Program Analysis and Evaluation)
- Bio-Systems Directorate, Human, Social, Cultural, and Behavior (HSCB) initiative (OSD DDR&E)
- Map-Human Terrain Tool or HSCB government off-the-shelf and commercial off-the-shelf (OSD Advanced Systems and Concepts)
- Integrated Behavioral Governance/Process Environment Capability (Defense Threat Reduction Agency (DTRA)/OSD (NII)/AT&L)
- Integrated Behavioral Capabilities (Joint Interagency Task Force-South, SOCOM)
- Social-Cultural Advanced Studies and Concept Office (DTRA)
- Bio-Chem Directorate, Cognitive Modeling (DTRA)
- Human Factors Analysis (DIA)
- Strategic Multilayer Analysis initiative (STRATCOM/OSD AT&L)
- Global Innovative Strategic Center / Human Network Attack Initiative (STRATCOM)
- RIO Strategic Centers. Foreign national military students conducting research on interoperability of their nation state. (OSD Policy/NII)
- Joint Task Center-Intelligence. Integration of intelligence efforts from the combatant commanders, coalition, and interagency. (JFCOM)

Modeling and Simulation

- TIARA (Sandia Labs and University of Mexico) (maturing)
- Modeling Phase-Change Behavior. Understanding the dynamics of group phenomena (maturing)
- Modeling Terrorist Recruitment and Motivation with Observable Indicators to identify sectors of societies of different socio-economic strata. (Indiana University/Purdue University, Fort Wayne, IN) (maturing)
- A Cultural Analysis of Three Afghanistan Provinces (Glevum Associates, LLC) (mature)
- Toward Systematic Social Modeling of counter-terrorism and counter-WMD (Krasnow Institute, George Mason University) (non-mature)

Table D-2. Current DoD Efforts, OSD Perspective (continued)

Field Application Efforts

- Human Terrain. Af ghan Support Team requested cultural analyses on three eastern provinces to provide data on current cultural landscape to predict reactions. (maturing)
- Integrated Behavioral Analysis Capability. The integration of HSCB assessments and visualized results. (DTRA/OSD NII)
- Manhunt. Manhunting Pilot Program on best practices, legal statutes, bounty hunting networks, development of training materials and procedures for employing manhunting techniques. (Combating Terrorism Technology Support Office/San Francisco (CTTSO/SF)–Technical Support Working Group (TSWG); Matrix Operating Solutions Research (prime contractor))
- Strategic Multilay er Analysis Initiative (STRATCOM/OSD AT&L Rapid Response Office)

Analysis Capability

- CALEB II. Tactical last mile targeting. A JIEDDO funded irregular warfare analysis capability that includes systems architecture, innovative TTP's, data modeling, and predictive analysis to provide a mature, tailored layer of analysis of insurgent operational networks and operating patterns. (CTTSO/SF– TSWG) (non-mature)
- Self-Organizing Groups Study. Research how self-organizing systems can be influenced from the external environment to support change or destroy belief structures. (CTTSO/SF– TSWG; The Rendon Group (prime contractor))(non-mature)

Appendix E. Computational Modeling for Reasoning about the Social Behavior of Humans

The number of models of human social behavior is growing rapidly. Unfortunately, the current ease of programming is turning adequate programmers into poor modelers capable of turning out tools with impressive interfaces, but little theoretical power under the hood. On the other hand, the plethora of new model-building toolkits is facilitating the rapid growth of simple proof of concept models. The current spate of models range from the simplistic to the elaborate, the conceptual to the empirical, and the purely notional to the ones that can be validated. This review briefly describes the current state of modeling and the relative strengths and weaknesses of the type of models now available. Key issues surrounding analysis and validation are discussed.

Introduction

Computational modeling, which is a growth area in the social and behavioral sciences, refers to any effort in which a model is realized as a set of computer code. These efforts include a computer program or network of computers and programs, that attempt to simulate an abstract model of the system. Such models are also referred to as computer simulation, computer models, and computational models. In a mathematical model, the relations are expressed in mathematical terms and processing is done by solving the equations. Computational modeling is a form of mathematical modeling, typically used when a closed form solution is not possible. In such a model the relations are expressed in mathematical or symbolic terms and processing is done by following an algorithm.

There are many types of computational models. Among the most common forms are agent-based models (also referred to as multi-agent systems), system dynamic models, and statistical forecasting. Reviews of computational models seek to characterize such models along a wide number of dimensions (Table E-1). While modeling frameworks typically fall in to one of these categories, models developed for adversarial reasoning that are not built in a framework are typically hybrids that criss-cross these boundaries at will.

Table E-1. Characteristics of Computational Models

Intellective versus emulative
Stochastic[76] versus deterministic[77]
Steady state[78] versus dynamic[79]
Continuous[80] versus discrete[81]
Rule-based versus equation
Learning versus static versus optimization
Centralized multi-agent versus distributed multi-agent
Local versus distributed[82]
System dynamic versus multi-agent versus multi-agent network

In comparison to traditional formal (*i.e.*, mathematical) models, computational models have the following characteristics:

- larger in scale—including more events, more actors, more entities, more time periods

- focus on the process and intermediate solutions and not equilibrium solutions (that are the key result of mathematical models)

- utilize a mix of simulated and real data as opposed to being completely algorithmic—for example, many computational models use simulated actors employing real equipment, or in real social networks

---

76. Stochastic models typically have at least one random number generation component.

77. A special case of deterministic models are the chaotic models.

78. Steady state models typically use a set of equations to define fixed relations.

79. In a dynamic system, relations among variables change in response to signals.

80. In a continuous system, periodically all equations are solved and state updated.

81. In a discrete system, a queue of events is maintained and only items related to the queue are solved.

82. In this case, local versus distributed refers to the hardware needed to run the computational model—a single machine (local) versus multiple machines (distributed).

- handle more complexity such as a greater number of interacting parts, higher levels of non-linearity in relationships, and very non-continuous response surfaces

As such, these models are often referred to as "complex system models." Finally, due to the usually stochastic nature of the results, impossibility of calculating a complete response surface, and attention to intermediate results, statistical analysis is typically used to provide an interpretation of model outcomes for computational models.

There are a number of reasons to use computational models in the area of human dynamics, including:

- **Ethical.** You cannot test the effects of policies on real populations but can on simulated populations.

- **Preparatory.** You can use these models to create hypothetical situations with more potency than existing ones. As a result, you can use the models to examine a wide range of scenarios. This enables more systematic imaginative thinking and facilitates training.

- **Cost effective.** Creating new technologies, procedures, and legislation for data collection is expensive; but, by using computational modeling, such things can be pretested for efficacy.

- **Faster.** Real time evaluation of existing systems is too time-consuming; however, in a simulation one can "speed up time," enabling rapid development and testing of alternatives.

- **Appropriate.** The world and the simulation are both complex non-linear dynamic systems. Hence the tool matches the requisite complexity and does not overly simplify the state, thus affording more accurate predictions and assessments.

- **Flexible.** Response to novel situations requires rapid evaluation of previously unexamined alternatives. This can be done best in a computational framework.

Computational models can be used for a number of purposes, including:

- test bed for new ideas

- predict impact of technology or policy

- develop theory

- determine necessity of a posited mechanism

- decision-making aids

- forecast future directions

- "what if" training tools

- suggest critical experiments

- suggest critical items for surveys

- suggest relative impact of different variables (factors)

- suggest limits to statistical tests for non-linear systems

- substitute for person, group, tool, etc. in an experiment

- hypotheses generators

Veridicality and Model Type

One of the key issues that drives the design, assessment, and validation of computational models is their level of veridicality.[83] On the one hand, many researchers would argue that Occam's razor should apply, and all models should follow the KISS principle (keep it simple stupid). Examples of models that employ a "proof-of-concept" approach are Sugarscape; many of the Santa-Fe institute models; many of the original "thought based" computational models, such as the Cohen March and Olson's garbage-can model, the Axelrod and later Sakoda's segregation model; and Kaufman's NK model. While others argue that to have strong policy relevance and to be able to use the model to make validatable claims, a higher level of veridicality is called

---

83. Veridicality is the extent to which a knowledge structure accurately reflects the information environment it represents.

for. Examples of such models include Carley's BioWar and Silverman's Athena Prism.

In general, the higher the level of veridicality the more types of problems the model can be used to address. In addition, these models have a larger amount of code. Although it is less likely the code is made available, it is more likely that aspects of the model can be validated. However, it is less likely that the model can be validated in full because it is less likely that the entire response surface can be generated. Finally, the higher the level of veridicality, the less likely the computational model will be built in one of the modeling frameworks available for system dynamic, agent-based, or event-based modeling, as the developers will need finer control over the development environment.

From a human behavioral standpoint, one key issue is how sophisticated or veridical is the model human agent in these computational models. In general, the higher the level of veridicality in the model human agent, the fewer agents are typically being modeled. Thus, multi-agent systems that have millions of agents typically have very rudimentary agents formed from only a few rules or equations that reflect very simple cognitive or social activities on the part of the agent. Simulations with thousands of agents tend to include fairly sophisticated and accurate parameters of human socio-cultural behavior. Simulations with less than a dozen agents are more likely to have very sophisticated cognitive and/or task models within the agents. In general, the higher the level of veridicality, the fewer the agents, the longer the model processing time for determining the actions of a single agent, and the greater the storage needs for a single agent.

One can achieve comparable storage and speed constraints as the level of agent veridicality is increased if the number of agents is reduced. In general, the tradeoff is that detailed cognitive processing and task-based behavior is often less present in models with thousands of agents, whereas social and cultural activity, and learning by being told, is less present in models with a small number of agents. Epstein and Axtell's Sugarscape uses millions of simple agents, Carley's Construct uses thousands of moderately veridical agents, and Act-R and Soar models typically use a handful of highly cognitively sophisticated agents.

Carley and Newell define three dimensions along which the model social agent varies: cognitive limitations, type of socio-cultural context knowledge, and amount of knowledge about the context. The amount of knowledge that the agent has might impact the speed of the computational model and the quality of the results but not the type of behaviors possible. In contrast, the other two dimensions impact the type of agent behaviors that it should be possible to generate from the computational model. The basic argument is that by placing appropriate limitations on agent cognitive activity and by placing the agents in, and giving them capability to recognize and respond to all classes of knowledge associated with a complete socio-cultural context, the agent model becomes the model social agent—a highly veridical avatar of human behavior in all situations. In general, most computational models use agents in less comprehensive environments or without appropriate cognitive limitations and as a result the agents cannot truly generate all human behaviors.

Figure E-1 illustrates where many current models fall on these dimensions. In the figure, each computational model (in italics) is placed in the cell furthest to the right and bottom that appears possible for the model. This means that a model in a particular cell, with its current architecture, should be applicable to any and all of the behaviors above and to the left of the cell by simply adding more knowledge. It is important to note that this breakdown is illustrative, not definitive. In addition, a key take-home message from the figure is that there is NO computational model today that has a highly veridical model social agent.

In addition to the lack of a good candidate for a model social agent, there are a number of limitations faced by computational models in the human social behavioral area at this point in time. One key limitation is that there is no single unifying theory of human social behavior. Rather, there are a panoply of theories, some of which lead to contradictory conclusions and all of which have received a limited amount of validation, though often only in a specific context. Another key limitation is that there is no single data set of sufficient detail, longitudinal nature, cross-cultural, and large enough in size to support validation of all aspects of any of the existing models, let alone models that might be developed in the future. The higher the level of veridicality in a computational model, the more "theories" of social behavior are embedded, at least implicitly, in the model.

Knowledge – Increasingly Rich Situation

	Nonsocial Task	Multiple Agents	Real Interaction	Social Structure	Social Goals	Cultural Historical
Omniscient	Goal directed Produces goods Uses tools Uses language	Models of others Turn taking Exchange	Face-to-face	Class differences	Organizational goals	Historically situated
Rational Agent	Reasons Acquires Learns	Learns from others Education Negotiation	Miscommunica-tion	Promotion Social mobility	Competition Cooperation Social cognition	Emergent norms *Seas Economic Models Cultural Transmission*
Boundedly Rational Agent	Satisfices Task planning Adaptation	Group making	Social planning Coercion Priority disputes	Altruism Uses networks for information Boundary spanners *Garbage Can Model Sugarscape, AAIS*	Delays gratification Moral obligation *RTE VDT TAEMS*	Gate keeping Role emergence *CORP, HITOP-A, ACTION, ORGAHEAD, Organizational Consultant*
Cognitive Agent	Compulsiveness Lack of awareness Multi-tasking	Group think	Spontaneous Exchange Social interaction *Soar*	Automatic response to status cues *Construct*	Group conflict Power struggles	Develop language Institutional change
Emotional Cognitive Agent	Habituation Variable performance	Protesting Trust *Athena*	Play Rapid emotional response Cons	Campaigning	Team player	Norm maintenance Ritual maintenance Advertising ***MODEL SOCIAL AGENT***

*(Vertical axis label: **Cognitive Architecture** – Increasingly Limited Capabilities)*

Figure E-1. Illustrative Classification of Activities and Models

Models, Metrics, and Social Networks

The term model typically refers to an abstraction of reality at the system level. In other words, within a model there are numerous variables that can take on a range of values, and these variables are linked together in some form of pattern of influence. The term metric typically refers to a measure with key mathematical properties, such as having a true 0 point and values having the transitivity property. A variable in a model can be a metric.

In the area of social networks, or network science, these terms are sometimes used interchangeably. For example, some refer to the metric, "betweenness," to characterize a social network model of power. Others refer to the network itself, or the graphic visualization of the network, as a model of the group, *e.g.*, a network where each link represents who interacts with whom among members of a small company might be referred to as the network model of that company. In this case, inherent in the "model" are a set of network properties of the nodes, *i.e.*, their value on a set of metrics. In still other cases, an agent-based model in which the agents learn from others to whom they are connected, or who alter their connections to others, or a system dynamics or event-based model that uses network metrics as variables are also referred to as network models. Hence, when the term network model is used, it behooves the reader or listener to understand how the term model is being used. From a computational perspective, for large networks with thousands of nodes, for example, many metrics cannot be calculated exactly in a reasonable amount of time and, therefore, heuristic-based computational approaches are used.

From a social behavioral modeling perspective, the area of social networks is of critical importance for four reasons. First, of all the computational modeling areas, the area of network science is the most developed. There is a set of well understood, validated, documented, and meaningful metrics; toolkits; well understood procedures for data collection and analysis; and social networks that are easily linked to other types of models. Second, networks constrain and enable behavior to the extent that understanding the network in a group is critical to identifying key actors and supports course of action analysis. Third, network metrics and models have been used with demonstrable success to support real world decisions in areas such as corporate re-organization, counter-terrorism, law-enforcement, and social policy. Fourth, there is a recognizable curriculum that individuals need to know to be competent in the social network area. In general, the most successful cases are those in which a meta-network approach was taken (see below). Unfortunately, the currently popularity of network science has led to a swell in the number of people claiming to do work in this area with most of the "practitioners" having little relevant background. As a result, recently there has been a tremendous amount of re-invention and re-discovery.

Networks constrain and enable behavior. In social networks (people-to-people), who interacts with whom, impacts what information is learned and transmitted, the flow of diseases, and the flow of money. However, networks impact more than just people. In many situations, it is important to think about the dynamics of meta-networks that connect the "who" (people and organizations), "what" (tasks, activities, and events), "where" (locations either at the general level—a building or a specific latitude and longitude), "why" (attitudes, beliefs, norms, goals) and "how" (resources and expertise needed to accomplish the "what" and held by the "who"). However, most network analysis tools focus only on social networks and/or utilize standard social network metrics on other networks without re-validating or determining if the metrics still make sense. A key exception here is the ORA tool which was designed from its inception to handle multi-mode multi-link dynamic networks—that is, meta-networks.

Network models are often touted as "data greedy." Because the model is of a group and the nodes are people, most accurate results require knowing for each pair of individuals whether or not they are connected. However, a network science approach can be used at any level, individual, group, state, or interstate. The nodes can be anything. The links can represent any number of types of relations. The links can vary in strength, directionality, and confidence. This being said, most network tools can only handle one to two types of nodes at a time (*i.e.*, one to two types of relations), and most metrics only operate on binary data where the links have been reduced to present or not. There are, however, a growing number of exceptions, such as ORA.

Terms of Reference

ACQUISITION,
TECHNOLOGY
AND LOGISTICS

DEC 2 2 2007

MEMORANDUM FOR CHAIRMAN, DEFENSE SCIENCE BOARD

SUBJECT: Terms of Reference – Task Force on Understanding Adversaries

Increased understanding of adversaries, their operating environment and the relevant host population is important to conduct complex operations (including stability, security, transition and reconstruction operations), to devise effective terrorist and insurgent countermeasures, to support strategic communications, and to aid intelligence analysis and planning for contingencies.

The Department of Defense (DoD) needs to understand the adversary and host population social structure, culture, motivations, beliefs, and interests that contribute to behavioral actions and responses. This understanding is necessary to recognize behavioral patterns and gain influence in interactions with host populations, friendly forces and potential adversaries (training, advising, crowd responses, patrolling, key leader engagements and other interactions). Our adversaries often have the advantage of local understanding and connections to host populations, as well as an effectively utilized understanding of Western thinking and cultures.

In the face of American dominance in traditional forms of warfare, we see new efforts among nations and non-state actors seeking to counter U.S. conventional superiority by making use of irregular tactics and campaigns for influence over local populations and institutions. Furthermore, there are many indications that they are doing better than us and are making significant gains in the eyes of their supporters. Ultimately, DoD and the United States may pay a high price for failing to understand their motivations and those of their supporters.

To improve understanding of adversaries and the populations in which they operate, the Task Force should:

- Review and re-evaluate previous and current attempts in DoD to assess host population social structures, culture, adversarial thinking styles and patterns of behavior.

- Identify and assess current relevant science and technology investment plans, to include research, analysis, tools and techniques.

- Identify new capability opportunities.

- Identify how relevant approaches, analysis, methods, technologies can be incorporated into U.S. military capabilities and systems (planning, intelligence, decision making, training, etc.).

- Identify mechanisms that may be needed to accelerate the transition of relevant approaches and tools into U.S. military capabilities.

- Develop recommendations to achieve operational capabilities.

Where relevant, the Task Force should draw upon the ongoing work of the OUSD(P)/OUSD(I) Human Terrain/Socio-cultural Analysis Integrated Process Team, the DDR&E Human Social Culture Behavior Modeling Program, and the OUSD(P&R) white paper on cultural and regional proficiency.

The study will be sponsored by the Acting Under Secretary for Defense for Acquisition, Technology and Logistics and the Under Secretary of Defense for Policy. Dr. Ann Skalka and Mr. Larry Lynn will serve as the Task Force Chairpersons. Mr. David Sobyra of OUSD(P) will serve as the Executive Secretary, and Commander Cliff Phillips, USN, will serve as the DSB representative.

The Task Force will operate in accordance with the provisions of P.L. 92-463, the "Federal Advisory Committee Act," and DoD Directive 5105.4, the "DoD Federal Advisory Committee Management Program." It is not anticipated that this Task Force will need to go into any "particular matters" within the meaning of title 18, U.S. Code, section 208, nor will it cause any member to be placed in the position of acting as a procurement official.

John J. Young, Jr.

2

Task Force Membership

CHAIRMEN

Name	Affiliation
Dr. Ann Skalka	Fox Chase Cancer Center
Mr. Larry Lynn	Private Consultant

MEMBERS

Dr. Randy Borum	University of Southern Florida
Dr. Kathleen Carley	Carnegie Mellon University
Gen Paul Gorman, USA (Ret.)	Former Combatant Commander
Dr. Mark Maybury	MITRE Corporation
Dr. Montgomery McFate	Institute for Defense Analyses
Mr. Robert Nesbit	MITRE Corporation
Mr. Sam Rascoff	New York University, formerly New York City Police Department
Mr. Mark Stout	Institute for Defense Analyses
Ms. Leigh Warner	Private Consultant

GOVERNMENT ADVISORS

CDR Sean Bigerstaff	Office of the Director, Defense Research and Engineering
Dr. Alenka Brown-Vanhooser	Office of the Assistant Secretary of Defense for Networks and Information Integration
Mr. Wade Ishimoto	Department of the Navy
M. R.C. Porter	Office of the Secretary of Defense
Mr. Ben Riley	Office of the Secretary of Defense

EXECUTIVE SECRETARY

Mr. Dave Sobyra	Office of the Under Secretary of Defense for Policy

DSB REPRESENTATIVE

CDR Clifton Phillips	Office of the Under Secretary of Defense for Acquisition, Technology, and Logistics

STAFF

Ms. Barbara Bicksler	Strategic Analysis, Inc.
Ms. Kelly Frere	Strategic Analysis, Inc.
Ms. Teresa Kidwell	Strategic Analysis, Inc.
Ms. Carla King	Strategic Analysis, Inc.

Presentations to the Task Force

Name	Topic
OCTOBER 29-30, 2007	
Mr. Steve Fondacaro Program Manager, G2 TRADOC	DoD Human Terrain System (HTS) Program
General Paul Gorman, USA (Ret.)	Theater Military Assistance and Advisory Group – Future (TMAAG-F)
Mr. Wade Ishimoto Office of the Deputy Under Secretary of the Navy	Special Operations Forces
Dr. Joseph Markowitz Private Consultant	Intelligence Requirements in the 21st Century
Dr. Vince Vitto Private Consultant and Vice Chairman of the DSB	Strategic Communication
Ms. Melissa Drisko Chief of Community Enterprise Operations DIA/Directorate for Analysis	Foreign Socio-cultural Dynamics and Defense Intelligence
NOVEMBER 26-27, 2007	
Mr. Robert Nesbit Senior Vice President and General Manager of MITRE Corporation	Combatant Commands Integrated Priority Lists
Dr. Jerrold Post Director of the Political Psychology Program at George Washington University	Deterring Asymmetric Rivals
LTC Benjamin E Webb (USA) Army G-3 Mr. William Chou Institute for Defense Analyses	The Unit Perspectives Project: Tactical Intelligence and the Iraqi Threat through Warriors' Eyes

Dr. Michael Wertheimer Assistant Deputy Director and Chief Technology Officer for Analysis at the Office of the Director of National Intelligence Dr. Jill Egeth MITRE Corporation	Summer Hard Problem (SHARP) Program
Dr. Montgomery McFate Institute for Defense Analyses	Socio-Cultural Requirements of Warfighters
Dr. Mark Maybury Executive Director, Information Technology Division, MITRE	Analytic Methodologies Used by the Intelligence Community
COL H.R. McMaster MAJ Daniel Barnard US Army	Counterinsurgency Operations and Understanding Adversaries

JANUARY 28-29, 2008

Dr. Jarrett Brachman Director of Research, Combating Terrorism Center (CTC), West Point	Combating Terrorism Center
Lt. Col. Todd Lyons Marine Corp Intelligence Activity	Marine Corps Intelligence Activity
Dr. Kathleen Carley Carnegie Mellon University	Computational Models for Adversarial Reasoning
Mr. Wade Ishimoto Office of the Deputy Under Secretary of the Navy Dr. Alenka Brown-Vanhooser Office of the Assistant Secretary of Defense for Networks and Information Integration	Ongoing Programs in DoD and Elsewhere
Steve Guthrie TRADOC, G-2	Army Culture and Foreign Language Strategy
Dan Butler Office of the Director of National Intelligence, Deputy Director for Open Source	Intelligence Collection Architecture

FEBRUARY 19-20, 2008

Dr. Joe Rosen Dartmouth-Hitchcock Medical Center	The Strategic Impact of US Casualties
Dr. John Chin President and CEO, Strategic Effects, LLC	Effects Based Cultural Intelligence for Operational Personnel
Nate Allen National Defense University	Company-Level Leadership in the Contemporary Operating Environment
Tom Rieger, Chris Steward, and Poppy MacDonald The Gallop Organization	Preventing Adversaries: Attitudes, Conditions and Barriers
COL David Maxwell G3, U.S. Army Special Operations Command	Perspectives on Understanding Host Populations: Education, Training, Studies, Methods and Tools

MARCH 17-18, 2008

Susan Brandon Counterintelligence Field Activity	Preliminary Credibility Assessment Screening System (PCASS)
Timothy Persons Intelligence Advanced Research Projects Activity	Human Terrain Research Portfolio
Dr. Montgomery McFate Institute for Defense Analyses	Human Terrain System Baghdad Assessment Team
Larry Wright Private Consultant	Islam and Fundamentalist Islam
Mr. Matt VanKonynenburt, Kelcy M. Allwein, and Nicole Sponaugle Defense Intelligence Agency	DIA Human Terrain Research

APRIL 28-29, 2008

Dr. Robert Foster Office of the Deputy Under Secretary of Defense (Science and Technology), DDR&E	S&T Investments in Human Dynamics-Related Programs
Michael Thompson DARPA COL Randy Dragon National Training Center (NTC)	National Training Center
Lt. Col Tommy Scott	Career Marine Regional Studies Program

JUNE 4-5, 2008

Dr. Sean O'Brian Defense Advanced Research Projects Agency (DARPA)	DARPA's Computational Social Science Portfolio
COL James Hickey, USA Institute for Defense Analyses, Joint Advanced Warfighting Program	Value of Cultural Understanding in Theater
Amy Kruse, PhD DARPA Program Manger	Career Marine Regional Studies Program

Glossary

ACR	armored cavalry regiment
ASD	Assistant Secretary of Defense
ASD (NII)	Assistant Secretary of Defense for Networks and Information Integration
AT&L	Acquisition, Technology, and Logistics
BCT	brigade combat team
CAOCL	Center for Advanced Operational Culture Learning
CTTSO/SF	Combating Terrorism Technology Support Office/San Francisco
DARPA	Defense Advanced Research Projects Agency
DCGS	Distributed Common Ground Station
DCO	Defense Connect On-Line
DDR&E	Director, Defense Research and Engineering
DIA	Defense Intelligence Agency
DISA	Defense Information Systems Agency
DOD	Department of Defense
DSB	Defense Science Board
DTRA	Defense Threat Reduction Agency
FAO	Foreign Area Officer
FM	field manual
HSCB	human, social, cultural, and behavior
HTS	Human Terrain System
ID	infantry division
IO	information operations
JFCOM	U.S. Joint Forces Command
JIEDDO	Joint Improvised Explosive Device Defeat Organization
MCIA	Marine Corp Intelligence Activity
M&S	modeling and simulation
MSOAG	Marine Special Operations Advisor Group

NGO	non-government organization
NII	Networks and Information Integration
NIPRNet	Unclassified but Sensitive Internet Protocol Router Network
OEF	Operation Enduring Freedom
OIF	Operation Iraqi Freedom
OSD	Office of the Secretary of Defense
P&R	Personnel and Readiness
PSYOP	psychological operations
QDR	Quadrennial Defense Review
RDEC	Research and Development Experimental Collaboration
RDT&E	research, development, test, and evaluation
ROTC	Reserve Officer Training Corps
SIPRNet	Secret Internet Protocol Router Network
SOCOM	U.S. Special Operations Command
SOF	Special Operations Forces
SSTR	stability, security, transition, and reconstruction
S&T	science and technology
STRATCOM	U.S. Strategic Command
TIGR	Tactical Ground Reporting
TOA	transfer of authority
TRADOC	U.S. Army Training and Doctrine Command
TSWG	technical support working group
UNOSUM	UN Operation in Somalia
USD (AT&L)	Under Secretary of Defense for Acquisition, Technology, and Logistics
USD (P&R)	Under Secretary of Defense for Personnel and Readiness
WMD	weapons of mass destruction